Praise for *Afterglow (a dog memoir)*

"Unflinching but also irrepressibly humorous. [Myles's] grief at losing Rosie is profound; it is also a revelation . . . Myles possesses, in abundance, two qualities of the highest value for a writer, irreverence and relentless curiosity, and here both are on full display . . . [*Afterglow*] is a love story, and because, like any serious book about death, it is full of life, it has a celebratory feel to it . . . By turns playful, heartfelt, wise, compassionate, fantastical and audaciously confessional."
—Sigrid Nunez, *New York Times Book Review*

"A wry, gorgeous, psychedelic effort to plumb the subject of dog-human partnership . . . An exceptional power struggle, a thought experiment about the limits of consciousness, creativity, and love . . . A punk devotional, shot through with a sort of divine attention to material reality and a poet's associative leaps."
—Jia Tolentino, *New Yorker*

"Myles gets at something no other dog book I've read has gotten at quite this distinctly: The sense of wordless connection and spiritual expansion you feel when you love and are loved by a creature who's not human . . . Raw and affecting, and in its wild snuffling way, utterly original."
—Maureen Corrigan, *Fresh Air*, NPR

"*Afterglow* portrays a complex and often hilarious relationship between two animals, characterized by love and deep interrogation of power, creativity, and point of view . . . For Myles, a dog becomes the surrogate for a sort of vicarious enlightenment . . . An ever-deepening investigation into the nature of human-being-ness, self-knowledge, and knowing things outside of yourself."

D0499607

"A work of surpassing strangeness that takes the form of an elegy for a lost pet and converts it into a weird and agitated philosophical inquiry into—well, love, life, death, the bardo states in between, plaid, pathetic art, Manichaeism, lost parents, animal vision, alcoholism, Ireland, gender, ecstasy and grief . . . Maybe this isn't a memoir, but a wild riff on authorship, especially the vexed business of how to get the world on to the page still wet."   —Olivia Laing, *Guardian*

"You'll laugh, and you'll cry, yes, but you'll also think hard, as you work to pull together the many disparate, cosmic, and charming notions Myles sets forth . . . Quicksilver intellect and whimsy."
                                                              —*Boston Globe*

"It is poetry, it is fiction, it is monologue and screenplay with diagrams and drawings. A dizzying pastiche standing on four legs, next to two."   —*Seattle Times*

"Warps the canon by embodying the mutability of memory and mind. At the crossroads of a book about the fading life of Myles's beloved pit bull, Rosie, is a blueprint for dismantling conformity and exploring the sublime planes of our existence."   —*Guernica*

"Eileen Myles is an estuary of a writer. The voice on the page is so fluid and expressive and unembarrassed that it makes you want to join it."   —*New York Times Magazine*

"[*Afterglow* aims] to catalog life in gritty, naturalistic stills that, when amassed over time, form a lyrical whole, like a good grunge song . . . Myles works to bridge the power discrepancies between owner and dog, author and subject."   —*Los Angeles Review of Books*

"Fantastical . . . Wrenching . . . Obsession becomes a way to process grief."   —*Rolling Stone*

"What is a dog if not god? In *Afterglow*, Eileen Myles steps up to the

mourning of the dog Rosie's death leads to surprising landscapes of thought in the language, where between sentences you're walking into vast open-air arenas and every time you do this some new light goes on in your brain. You think you're reading about Eileen and a dog. You are reading about them, but with the complexities of their closeness always pointing farther up the field, asking why we're here, what we're going to do and with whom are we going to do it."

—Renee Gladman, author of *Calamities*

"Wildly inventive and just plain wild, feral, even, Eileen Myles's dazzling *Afterglow* is about a dog, and her owner, and everything else in life, and also death, too."

—Jami Attenberg, author of *The Middlesteins* and *All Grown Up*

"To read Eileen Myles is to feel as if the poet, after spotting you across the room at a crowded party, has guided you by the elbow to a private corner to confide their personal theories of the universe. *Afterglow* is just that intimate. Part elegy, part meditation, part performance art . . . Poignant, sweeping."   —*O Magazine*

"It's about consciousness, grief, and love, and what it means to not just experience these states but to probe and reshape them, to ultimately (hopefully) reach some peace."   —*BuzzFeed*

"Myles's storytelling is as unconventional and allusive as ever, ranging from an imaginary talk show featuring Rosie as a guest to the more quotidian joys of loving an animal."   —*Elle*

"Dazzles in unexpected ways. Myles weaves together seemingly disparate topics and personal vulnerabilities to advance their store to a sense of possibility. Their signature brand of rawness, delivered with their Boston vernacular and punk tenacity, renders their grief different from a conventional memoir . . . Myles's prize-winning literary enigmatologist skills make this memoir an unapologetic, frisky tapestry, robust with canine energy."   —*Electric Literature*

challenge for writers to function as prophets. Ghostwritten in part by deceased pit bull Rosie, this 'dog memoir' explores—among other things—geometry, gender, mortality, evil, aging, and plaids. Myles makes new rules for what prose writing can be. *Afterglow* is Myles's funniest, profoundest work yet."

—Chris Kraus, author of *I Love Dick* and *After Kathy Acker*

"Part eulogy, part homage, part love-letter, part madcap scrapbook . . . Love and loss are replayed and reimagined through the paranormal and surreal just as against the everyday and the earthly; the familial, communal, spiritual, sexual and bestial are all enlisted to spin the story of one special canine and her human. Only Eileen Myles could reinvent the memoir again so stunningly; *Afterglow* is the sort of multidimensional love story you could only expect from one of our greatest experimental writers living today!"

—Porochista Khakpour, author of *The Last Illusion* and *Sick: A Life of Lyme, Love, Illness, and Addiction*

"Following Eileen Myles around a dog is like following Leopold Bloom around Dublin. Reading *Afterglow* is like entering the company of a sensibility that is rich, original, witty, and tonally brilliant. It is the darting asides, the phrasing and the subplots that matter most in this book, that give pure, sheer constant pleasure."

—Colm Tóibín, author of *House of Names*

"Everything Eileen Myles touches turns to poetry. Whether called a dog or a cat, it's always poetry. Emily Dickinson famously decided that poetry was anything that made her 'feel physically as if the top of my head were taken off.' I can imagine Emily Dickinson writing an ecstatic blurb for Myles's tender, trippy, deep, yet humanely silly new gift to the world: *Afterglow*. In this age of fake news and even fake poetry, trust this voice!"

—Brad Gooch, author of *Smash Cut* and *Rumi's Secret*

"What astounds me about *Afterglow* is the way in which Myles's

AFTERGLOW

(a dog memoir)

Also by Eileen Myles

Evolution

I Must Be Living Twice: New and Selected Poems 1975-2014

Snowflake / different streets

Inferno (a poet's novel)

The Importance of Being Iceland / travel essays in art

Sorry, Tree

Tow (with drawings by artist Larry R. Collins)

Skies

on my way

Cool for You

School of Fish

Maxfield Parrish / early & new poems

The New Fuck You / adventures in lesbian reading (with Liz Kotz)

Chelsea Girls

Not Me

1969

Bread and Water

Sappho's Boat

A Fresh Young Voice from the Plains

Polar Ode (with Anne Waldman)

The Irony of the Leash

AFTERGLOW

(a dog memoir)

EILEEN MYLES

Grove Press
New York

Published simultaneously in Canada
Printed in the United States of America

This book was set in Adobe Garamond Pro by
Alpha Design & Composition of Pittsfield, NH

First Grove Atlantic hardcover edition: September 2017
First Grove Atlantic paperback edition: September 2018

Library of Congress Cataloging-in-Publication data is available for this title.

ISBN 978-0-8021-2855-3
eISBN 978-0-8021-8878-6

Grove Press
an imprint of Grove Atlantic
154 West 14th Street
New York, NY 10011

Distributed by Publishers Group West

groveatlantic.com

18 19 20 21   10 9 8 7 6 5 4 3 2 1

for Genevieve Hannibal

Contents

AFTERGLOW
(a dog memoir)

EiLEEN MYLES
308 W. 40th st #2
NY, NEW YORK 10018

One day, in 1999, an awkward hand-addressed letter appeared in my hallway.

The mailman threw everything on the stairs. I grabbed the letter & headed with Rosie to the dog run which in that neighborhood was a skimpy little triangle at 39th Street west of 9th Ave. It was an amazing perspective on mid-town roofs and also dull traffic heading to New Jersey. My neighbors were weird. Sad former actors. I liked the pink-cheeked older woman named Doris who walked everyone in the neighborhood's dogs including mine. This is like sixteen years ago so Doris is probably dead. Sitting on a bench while Rosie sniffed the ground I tore open the strange note. It read:

Dear Eileen,

I take the liberty of calling you "Eileen" to begin the unpleasant duty of forcing you to legally take responsibility for the damages you have inflicted over a period of nine years upon the being you have taken to calling "Rosie." I am Rosie's lawyer. Dog lawyers have only become possible in recent years, even months. Which is not to say crimes of all kinds against dogs are "new" in any way. Crimes against dogs are ancient and widespread, but dogs having the wherewithal to attain legal representation is new indeed. My services have been retained thanks to a generous bequest by an anonymous donor who set up a foundation in her will for the explicit purpose of identifying dogs who were likely litigants, candidates for beginning the long and arduous process of getting the ball rolling on dogs' rights. It's been clear to my client during her life and most pressingly at the time of her death that the best way to make this need known would be to take up an individual dog's case, not the case of "all dogs" which is too ubiquitous to pursue in the explicit way the law makes possible for human litigants, who are generally assumed to be individuals. A wealthy individual, of course, does not have more rights than a poor one. We are all brought up to honor "human rights," but only wealthy humans are able to use the full force of the law; i.e., obtain high quality representation. By this logic, there can be no freedom for dogs unless there are wealthy dogs. There is one today, the dog formerly known as Rosie. She has been left a significant sum of money in my client's will. She may spend it as she pleases with the single stipulation that she obtain counsel and press charges against her owner for a variety of abuses and crimes against dog kind. As you know, Eileen Myles, that owner is you.

It seemed unbelievable to me. Rosie was about ten. I looked at her licking an empty wrapper against the fence. She appeared entirely innocent of the letter's content. *What?* Are we already going home she seemed to say. Okay. I don't think she knows anything about this. I popped the leash back on and walked home planning my day. The loft we lived in was right across from Port Authority. Day and night I watched the lights of buses sail in and out of the building. I thought about the letter from time to time. I mean for years. I showed it to people. They laughed and smiled. Could Rosie and my entire relationship be framed as blame. I did force her to have sex with Buster that one time. No twice. Could I write a book about that. I've never been an "idea" writer. I have like a spurt then I go do something else. But this would be her book. A dog book is a great idea . . .

Protect Me You

September, 2006

You've just fallen down on the grass. I thought this would be a nice place to sit in the afternoon. The cat shows up, black, looking out. When I'm surrounded by trees, a condition I've sought out pretty persistently throughout my life, the thing I think I might like the most about them is this whisper like all the hair of the world passing through the tunnel of one single breath—if that is a form of percussion. This irregular hiss of trees and wind. I think it is my mother. And I am her son, and you are my dog.

Our relationship is part discomfort & humiliation and part devotion. Oh once upon a time I wanted a dog exactly as much as I wanted to be alive. Maybe I didn't even want a dog then. I wanted to say that I was alive. Even to be a dog would be enough and how good if I could be seen wanting one and could begin asking for it incessantly—if I could summon up asking in every possible manner. Please. Leaving notes under pillows and toilet seat covers. Did I want a dog, really. No I

was a kid who was desperate to be seen in a state of desire &
supplication. That was many years ago. I wanted to already be
my yes. A positive child in a state of knowing & reaching out.
Not for myself but towards a friend. The child was denied. In
the manner of my family they said yes and then they said no.
Somewhere there is a picture of this. A little boy in bangs and
a plaid cotton shirt. (I remember it was red but the picture
was taken with my father's Polaroid land camera which took
black & white photos then which added to the beauty of them
because the past is so often a place whose colors are only in
my mind.) How hard it would be to be a movie star. To be in
full color in front of everyone. To be applauded and owned.
Isn't that like being a very good dog. You're lashing out at
photographers who are adamant about capturing you, your
every movement again and again. I admit I've wanted to be a
movie star to be seen in that disgraceful and hungry way—the
buttered toast of everyone. There I am with my beautiful smile.
A big piece of bread. Angry, covering my face. I held my dog
in the black and white world and I knew that this was the
moment I had wanted so keenly. To be still, to be fixed, to be
sad. I was just like a little prayer card holding my dog. I would
never know myself as clearly again.

Did that dog go on to her death when we returned her to
the ASPCA after that one long crying night that disturbed
my mother to no end. A tree will push this way and that be
permanent in its breath of time. It's hardly the color it is, a
white pole, some green some red. I would think a tree would
know exactly what it was and be so peaceful. As long as she's
breathing a dog is not at rest. So I was a child who wanted a

dog. I became myself. I certainly wasn't thinking I wanted a dog the day we met. I was watching the rollers turn. I mean time. You have to touch on something repeatedly but what could it be? How could that happen if time was your problem. What could you touch?

That's why I'm a poet. Even in the bathtub as a child I was syncopating my blubs because I didn't know what to do with the light and the wetness and my mother and when would it stop. I had a horror of life's never ending-ness which made me really hate art. Its spectacles. Rodeos. Circuses. People skating around on ice. And in the world on ponds. My feet hurt. And look—all the trees have lost their leaves and are black. Isn't it time to go in? It seems like the people around me wanted to do happy things and a child is supposed to be a little dog and bark happily in response—at the ice & the trees & the day. And now here it is all around us.

This morning I was reading in the paper how the governor of New Jersey a secret gay man had hired a poet of all the ludicrous persons on earth to be his director of homeland security. And then the poet realized the governor wanted him. How unabashedly corrupt of a governor to entice a total fool—a poet—practically a clown's occupation to take care of the people of a state. The state of New Jersey at that. The governor wanted the poet to hold him and love him and kiss his toes. Possibly the governor wanted to exercise his dominance over the poet shoving his penis in the poet's butt. I had already heard parts of this story, mostly about the governor's secret gayness, but it seems like they saved this one tiny detail for the end. The fact that the young man was appointed to a position in which he could only reveal his incompetence—who could blame him for that. He was young after all. But the later, more laughable tidbit. Like the room stopped laughing and then the little dog lifts its butt and poops. Homeland security! How could a poet do that. How could a *poet* do that. Twice a fool. And twice the governor's crime.

And speaking of such—now that we've seen really good photos of how really bad it was in New Orleans and we've seen also that the man in charge there, Brownie, knew about horses, not safety, there were problems really much bigger than his unknowing, the unknowing is always getting larger, and we've looked at them all publicly together, and realize that there are always people of greater authority equally incompetent people like the president who once owned a baseball team and now laughed publicly at a woman, Aileen, he whinnied at her who was being sent (by him) just then to the electric chair—he mocked her.

And supposedly when he was governor, he actually improved schools that was his big claim but now we've learned that in fact the books were cooked, that's all. And the schools got even worse under him and when he was a kid he used to blow up squirrels and he farts in front of his interns today—kids who went to good schools and studied hard—I'm not particularly impressed by those leadership types living or dead, maybe if one gets shot or mugged you see the kid's picture in the paper and think—what a shame he or she got good grades. But say he survives—winds up delivering papers to the oval office and there's the president laughing & farting. And you tried hard & he hadn't and now he's your boss and you've got to smell his farts. You're a dog.

The final insult to everyone was that what little New Jersey had to protect itself with was a poet. There's a little red up in the trees. And my dog wants to go upstairs. And I probably should let her have her way. Because she is dying.

Not only are her legs stiff, but her joints are swollen and covered with sores. I don't have another life partner. It's almost five decades after the perfect photograph of my desire and because Rosie's pacing all over the house and slobbering her food the ants are swarming around her like candy. She's a sweet dying clump. Today is the day when summer turns into fall. Surely the light is shorter or longer today. My planet is in some angle to the sun so that people say this is September a beautiful month when it's not too hot, possibly the sweetest time of the year. There are already waves and waves of what I am saying. I've set something in motion I can return to again and again. Anywhere. Dogs begin barking. You have never been a barker unless you were left outside a café tied to a post, then you yelped like hell. You like company.

I do too. I've discovered I'm an essentially social person. I like to sit in groups, or move with them. I like when they all decide to go see some art or celebrate the number of years a person's been on the planet. I even like when they all get loaded in honor of that. Though I get out of the room fast. I go for the rebounding energy of heys and hugs and awkward kisses and the opportunity to raise my flag and see it light up in your eye. Your flag tells me where I want to go next. It's like the world I live in is a field of flags whapping and waving and I want to see them all waving. I want to stand in the crowd or the small group. I like the small and large crowds that talk about how they feel. Who listen to one another, who let the collective listening and talking build up a head of swarming energy that fills and delights us. These are the groups that show me that I do like groups. I like to be alone. But then I need to talk to someone. I like god. When I was a child I was taught that there was someone listening and I chanced tiny hellos that frequently felt empty but longer conversations often silences felt like I was sitting in an enormous radio, like I had big headphones on when I felt separated from the world but tuned in to this show. And that's where you came in. Whether you listen or not, you're in there too. My dog. You're a part of the great silent show of this morning's sun. Turns out it was the most even day of the year, one of the two when dark and light counter balance each other. I have a round board in my house with balls underneath and I climb on while I'm waiting for water to boil or trying to escape the pressure inside, not god but a kind of weather I inhabit & control. I think it comes from Ireland which is why I feel I need to live there for a few years. I will. Just to understand the minerals and substances that spawned me. I come from Poland too but I live with Poland. This is Poland. Ireland is the mystery, Ireland is gone but like magic, it calls me home. I get on the board in my house it's in the kitchen so there's a square window. When I was a child we lived across the street from the ocean. It was a perfect spot. I learned to make sandwiches for myself in that house. That was adolescence. Squeezing a pepper and making it spurt. Eating my own food with you. In the sun. At last my life had begun. I had one job which was to do the dishes after dinner with my young arms and there was a stone church outside the window its bell. Sounds spreading out and landing in the marsh.

Up on my board I look out the window in my kitchen. That animal glance is enough. To connect me to the first suns, the first light and jobs. To be in and out within the reach of square light. The round board at first seeks to confound me. One orientation is pure reaching forward so you attempt to not tip yourself, not quite jerking back but asking a wave not to curl and you beg by little movements of your hip. Another, the side to side orientation demands that you use some bell inside your crotch to ring in the middle so to speak and there is a glorious feeling of hip no dick sway it makes me want to dance, and my calves planted and working, working continually. I discovered a new direction the other day I mean I had always been aware that the board made me TALL. It was simply that and there were people I wanted to be tall around and I mostly accomplish that with boots but you know boots aren't really for walking they're for promenading so you're going around in stilts in a way. You won't fall but when you think about them, and for all the pleasure of being a little higher the trade-off is your own absence from presence. You're losing your own fealty to the ground. Which can't be ignored. You lose your earth for your sky. When I'm on the board in my kitchen, when I get still, just for a click I am high—I think <u>oh</u> . . .

My Dog/My God

People said you'll know when I asked them how they knew it was time. When it was okay to take your dog's life. You'll know they said looking me right in the eye. And I did.

Rosie began dying in June, having those mysterious fits. At the end of each was a puddle of piss. I went to my meeting on Adams Ave. in the evenings and I talked about it. The one near the park with the working people: the beautiful dog walker, the pale curly haired man who taught law and came in covered in sweat, almost naked from running. One night he & I stood on the sidewalk under those shady trees. He said my name is Philip, lover of horses. He smiled. I thought he was flirting with me but it was part of his euphoria. I understood. Because I was the one with the dying dog. My friend the older woman said you've got to stop. I was biting my fingers. My dog is dying. I kept saying it. I wash her ass and then I wash all the towels. One evening I was feeling a little extra naked after describing the ritual of mopping her piss and I thought that's it. She's god. And I felt so calm. I've found god now. My God—My Dog. I chuckled. That's it. *Our room. This is ecstasy*

& everything got bright. She's dying & I'm watching her. I'm not *thinking* about it. Not that that makes any difference. I got this intention. This understanding. Did anyone ever say suffering was about difference. It sops it all up. We are this picture of ourselves now, Rosie and I and we want to be seen.

I took such care of her when she was dying. I relished it. She made me go slow. I'd hear the rustling of her limbs and I'd run to her because she couldn't get up and there was generally a puddle already there. In my house I have beautiful wooden floors. Now I had a pile of facecloths, torn towels, rags. I'd mop up her urine with a clean dry towel and then I'd come back and wash her ass. I'd come back with a damp one, wash it again and then I'd wipe her dry. I made sure she was really comfortable. I'd do it with love. I attended my dog's ass, the collapse of her rear legs that I saw as little high heels. I imagined her a drag queen or a young girl unsteadily teetering. A touching failure. I swooped in and made it better, made it comfortable. I felt loving. I felt like a god too. I felt less ambivalently loving than I have ever felt in my life. Now I know what love feels like. I do it and I think it. I love feeling this. Love loving your doggy ass. My home became a shrine. The bird of paradise around the door. The late night and early morning dog barking in the dark canyon beyond the yard. When I bought the house it said on the deed: disclosures. "Dogs in canyon." What could that mean. Hundreds and hundreds of dogs barking day and night. Not all the time. Just when any one of them got an idea. Then they all got it.

There's a growly picture of me standing in the screened-in porch light flooding in over that canyon and I look like an

animal. But the animal looks great. You see a movie sometimes in which someone is doing something really difficult, waging war, defending their family, walking very far, and very long and they look terrific, they look great. The hair looks good, the person looks well, they look hot. And I would watch these spectacles with a doubleness. I'd keep watching cause unless a movie is really bad I'm usually enthralled but I always think no one would look so good doing that. But in fact people often look radiant suffering. How often have you told someone they look fabulous and they say thanks cause I feel terrible. And you can see it right behind their eyes. Terrible puts a candle in there. Terrible turns on the light. You wonder if people are just empty when they're moving forward with the plan. When it's all on the outside and the world is full of light, but when you suffer the light is <u>in</u>. It's all yours.

I'd mop the floor after I took care of her body and I'd wash the animal print rug. The sound of the washing machine churning was a huge part of the day. And I felt it deeply. The expensive cost of water. On the west coast you are living on this shaky shelf that's gonna get choked. Everyone knows one day will come when there won't be any water. California is crazy. Water's getting sucked there through those long pipes from Colorado or someplace. Where *are* they getting this water from. I think Colorado is it. Some underground world slowly getting poisoned. Or drained. It's all very thin and it's going to end soon.

But we're spending the end of your life together. That is our vacation, our purpose. First Myra came and stayed with me and she agreed it was hard. I can't believe you're doing this & alone she said. I know but I love it I said. I understand she twinkled. Myra's around 50. It's interesting to see your friends grow old and when I say she twinkled I mean the moment Myra smiled all the versions of her were twinkling right at that moment. It's not just the dying who are filled with light. Myra was smiling from her experience which was cute. It was a light from far away, from many places, arriving here now.

Watching Rosie die made me a little in love with the whole wash of light, of time, its twists which must be why I ended it with Paige who visited me next. She was a young Canadian artist, and I met her at an opening in New York in the midst of a crowd of people all her age mostly female which is just like this world in San Diego where I'm living except in New York there's not a school. Here there's *millions* of young women. I almost can't see the young. They're like the greenness and the sky and the beach. Paige comes up to me at the opening. Are you <u>you</u> she goes. Ten years ago someone told me you're the only one your age who goes out. Now *they* don't go out. They're gone. People turn and look at me and say she's here. I'm like a breeze, I'm like punctuation on a text which is them. Which is why I am grateful to be home in California with my dog who is dying. Who is now dead.

California has great dog beaches. There was one in particular I was very fond of which was next to a naval base. You'd get to the end of the road and turn to park but there was this guard building and a guy in uniform standing right in front of it with a gun. Behind him the giant base perched on the beautiful beach with the ocean rocking all around—an island in California and we'd be driving there over the dazzling bridge from the mainland—you with your nose sniffing out the rear window—the window that when open produces what I think of as the convertible effect.

The most perfect thing about being there is that it is an island. You can feel it most of all at night. When you walk around the air comes from every direction and it reminds me of P-town, of those bars on Commercial Street in the summer. Here all that beauty and sexiness is owned by the military which is strange. The air in Provincetown was prowling around us inside and out and you could hear things not far away, knocking in the water, old, clunking and honking.

That one dimly lit music club that was open to the street. You could see the wind rock the orange lamps inside. Inside it reminded me of something else, all the air. Is it necessary for there to be a first air—an air that simply is yours? A place supremely young and old where you've spent your whole life. Growing up dying, going down to the beach, drinking, kissing. Are there people who have never lived in their air. Is this mine. I have never been one of a pair of young lovers, a young couple—but this air is mine. I know my air. Drifting, never landing, a life at sea. The sounds and the smells of that restless night, the lights, the feel—a body, if an animal didn't need a body. A drift.

I'm thinking of the beach I used to bring you in the morning —really early, about <u>nine</u>. About twelve years ago. The light was magical. It was just you and me and one fag—a waiter and he was swimming nude. It was his ritual. My own shirt was off—it was an abandoned part of the beach in a pretty gay town. All the other women were way on the other side of the beach. I liked this loner set up and I felt I was more than a bit of a man. A friend of mine used to have a crush on this waiter in New York. He had a kind of over-developed upper lip like a duck and he was slim and combed his hair back in a classic old-fashioned style. Not extravagant at all, but he was hip in a continental way. The fact that he could be with me on this beach in another city almost fifteen years later and not recognize me at all made me comfortable. It was like family. I had my dog and I had him who didn't know me. I have a striped towel—orange and dark blue. One of two. I buy one, forget it and buy another one. You'd think it was a straight town now. The beach is littered with couples and people with kids. Some man flies his kite delightedly and I want to say hey can you please go back the other way, you are taking way too much space. Yet I think it's wrong to talk to people like that. I can leave—go to the gym I think staring at the dunes. I can go walk the street looking for people to have dinner with. Then I put my nose in my notebook and I'm writing again.

Save.

The problem with getting Rosie to the beach on the little military island is that you have to walk *here* from way back down there cause the beach is right here by the guy with the gun. So the dog would have to be able to walk that far and this dog can't. This dog has become a puppet in her own life. I lift her up and talk to the dog head she is now. The permanently alive dog breathing in here. In fact I'm writing this book to *keep* talking to her.

Paige came to visit (I told her it's not going to be a vacation, she said very seriously I know) and she would get out with the dog at the mouth of the beach and I would go park and then join them. At some point sitting on the beach in the morning it seemed like maybe about a hundred guys in crew cuts went by running. She took a picture. She smiled at me and shrugged. It was the army training on the beach. I thought of her being Canadian. This was a whole other kind of beach.

After you died I went over there and I heard on the radio that the president George Bush was there and I stuck my head out the window and started screaming at people. He's a killer don't you know. Then I realized I couldn't go there anymore. You know they took Emma Goldman's boyfriend out in the desert here and anally raped him. The San Diego paper said they should do it to her too. It's *still* that paper. That's why I was so mad. He's my president too.

She changed suddenly that week. We went up to LA for the weekend cause there was nobody left in San Diego she could stay with. It was getting harder and harder to find anyone to stay with a dying dog. I'd call this one and she'd refer me to that one. Since about June which was when the fits began I'd wake up every morning thinking about it and unable to plan the future because of it not knowing where to be and frankly also feeling a little chased out of town by all the different kinds of young women. I felt overwhelmed by them. A college town is like totally bugged. You can't be old. You can't be invisible. You're just walking around being lonely. That's why everyone's married. You're either wrapped or unwrapped. There's too much youth. That's the job. It's too erotic. I came with someone and it didn't last. I had you.

So we took you up to LA for the weekend with us. And there was a dog lady you could stay with. She reminded me of the couple with a kid on E. 7th Street you stayed with when you were a puppy. This lady just had dogs, maybe cats too. No husband just animals. Cushions all around. You looked a little stunned when we left. It was just for the night and then we took you home.

How was she. She wouldn't eat dog food. She just had steak. The woman shrugged. Like it was cute. She must've liked that we laughed. To be an animal owner you get to be broad. Even a little deceitful. Nobody can speak up for herself. It's like an eternally silent child. Who you trust. Who shouldn't trust you. Who just keeps playing with the same ball and likes the same walk and is getting old.

We stopped off at that great place in San Juan Capistrano and got food and you had your own little taco. That was fun. We all ate in the car and drove home. I don't remember being happy. It was dark. I remember being full. We were all in the car. It was nice, everyone had food and we drove down the coast.

These places are all catholic places. San Diego. San Luis Obispo. I think of the monks who started the missions and the story they told us in school about the monks having boiling water poured on their heads. The Native Americans were making a joke. It was that one detail they taught us forever.

That first night Paige was gone I was standing out in the front yard in my bvds holding up your ass in a puddle of piss. It was like dawn. It was all night long. It kept happening. And my arm hurt and your legs were gone and I thought we can't do this anymore.

You would not eat dog food. Never again. You would only eat sausages and little steaks. And meanwhile you no longer would shit. You would never shit again for the rest of your life. She'll shit on the other side. That was my joke. Meanwhile I can no longer eat these sausages you get in health food stores that you liked because they remind me of your turds. Your whole insides aching, waiting for relief.

I went out on Friday night to read in that sex shop in North Park with the big back room where things happened. You were so quiet when I left. You were barely breathing. You were almost gone. There was this ottoman at the window where you were lying. You were so still.

Before Paige left she lowered the bed. To make it easier for you to get up cause you couldn't jump. But it was like changing the world and she won't be in it long. I remember thinking that. I liked it low for a while.

I used to clean this woman's house in New York. Years before. Her cat died and the cat was in bardo on the bed when I cleaned. I worked with this guy David who got me the job who died of AIDS and he said go look in the bedroom. It somehow made the house feel very good when we cleaned. Having a dead body in there.

I like to make it heavier sometimes. Saying versions of the same thing. I mean here. You probably already guessed it but I like saying it again. That one little piece again with a twist. And a thud. I don't feel this way about everything but there are moments that need to be heavy. As a fact. Not an idea.

When I got the puppy when I was a kid my father said go in the bedroom Eileen. It was my mother and father's bedroom where I was never allowed so I hated him telling me to do it. It didn't make sense. It scared me. Go in the bedroom, Eileen. The little dog walked out.

I read for Rosie that night. Read every poem she was in.[1] Dedicated it to her. Not that she needed it. She did not need poetry.

---

1. Note: We should do a little pamphlet of Rosie's poems.

She was it. Mainstay of my liturgy for sixteen point five almost seventeen years. She was observed. I was companioned, seen.

I read a long one about dogs I wrote before I ever even had one. It was about attachment. How I wanted it. Needed it. Least I had habits said the poem since I didn't have a dog. There was one about walking on the beach with a dog and hearing things. Hearing old people groaning as they walked in the sand. One was about counting things when I walked her. Almost losing her once. The color of her leash. My friend dying and its color getting mixed up with that. Her leash was so important. I started assigning numbers to each of the colors of the world like it was a paint-by-numbers that year before she was dying. I filmed her too. I was scared. The painting was fading. I was having my religion torn from me. Her body smelled corny. Her fur smelled like corn to me always and I never bathed Rosie till she was sick. I bathed her if she rolled in shit or dead fish. That was her P-town trick. & I never washed a floor. Not in my life, in all my worlds I never looked down. She had sores on her body all her life. All the puppies in her litter had bumps on their bodies. I got worried but after a while I'd just leave them there. I had a girlfriend who thought that was cruel. I went to the vet when I had money. You died when I had money. Most of the other puppies in your litter died. There was Africa who was last seen running between parked cars, scared. He was with that cute young couple but they must have abandoned him. There was "38", who someone in the neighborhood found and dropped off at the pound. What's going to happen to him now the guy

asked as he was leaving. Gas said the woman at the counter.
No one wants a pit. What cage is he in asked the guy. 38. He
went back and got him. We used to see 38 all the time. There
was Buster who lived in Tompkins Sq. Park with a homeless
kid. We saw him sometimes then I heard he ate rat poison
and died. Point is that I am a fucking saint. There was your
mother Lucy, white with a handful of pale black spots who
lived with the restaurant woman on 4th street, then Lucy was
gone. We used to see her up on the fire escape all the time.

I needed to talk to you about things. This was in the fall. You
died in December. I heard about this woman who could communicate with animals. I was having dinner with two friends
one from the west coast one from the east and they had both
heard of such a woman and it turned out she was the same
one. That's good.

Rosie's in California, I'm in New York the woman is in western
Mass. The way we do it Dawn Allen said is you tell me what
you want me to ask her. It's going to be silent on the line for a
few minutes because I'll be talking with her. I'll tell you what
Rosie has to say for herself.

Dawn came back giggling. This is an amazing dog. I've never
heard a dog talk this way before. She's quite a little poet. Oh
she must have known everyone says. I don't know. My question
was <u>what</u> was keeping Rosie around. She likes the smell of the
world. She likes the feeling of the wind on her fur. She likes
grass. She loves San Diego. She's very happy there.

She says she'll cross that bridge when she comes to it in reference to moving to LA. That's my family's talk. I knew it meant she wouldn't be there. It's how we say no.

When I came in from the reading she was on her hassock by the window. Again very still. I had to stare to catch her breathing. I crouched down. We've been together for a while I said. If you're ready to go it's okay. I got down with her eye to eye. It was grey. I felt like she was swimming in some fluid and I was in there with her. It was our intimacy. A silent place. I felt I was guided by her. Her deep prescient calm. I would miss her so much. I wanted to keep swimming with her. But I couldn't help it. I pulled out. I had to say no. I'm not dying with you. But who will I be without my dog. And I carried you to the bed.

The Death of Rosie

In the morning she felt very still. I felt like I could pick her up like a little football and pass her through. She hadn't moved all night.

I called the vet. It was Saturday morning. What's it like in there now. It's very quiet but you better get in here fast.

I called Ali and Anna who said they would come. <u>Were</u> <u>coming</u>. We need coffee. I grabbed her and my sleeping bag. I carried her, rolled up. I put her in the car.

There's a few ahead of you said Marcy as we came in. That's okay. I'm waiting for my friends. Why don't you take her into the corner said Marcy who was one of the people who stayed with her. Everyone in the animal world has a little business. They work at a vet's and they have dog walking cards on the counter.

Why now she asked, stroking Rosie's head. She was stooped down on the floor with us.

You don't think she's ready?

We've all been waiting for you. It is time.

The room kept filling. All the people with their young cats and dogs watching us in our sorrow. Did you know what was going on? Anna and Ali blew in. Rose Anna said crouching down. Is there anything we can do. Has she eaten? What would she like—How about some carne asada, Rose would you like that. Anna waved the money off. I'll be right back. Oh Rose said Ali her face growing big.

Anna fed Rosie the whole serving by hand. Rosie's eyes were large, bugged out like the only parts of her alive were the screaming whites of her eyes, the dark flat irises and her mouth. Prayerful but getting it down.

OK said the vet opening the door. It was Doctor Todd the old one. So it's time huh Rose. Do you think I'm rushing her. This is the hardest thing in the world she said ponderously but in her heart. My partner and I put our boy down a few months ago. It was the hardest thing we've ever done and we've lost a few. She's been ready for a while. It was you that was holding on. She didn't need to hang around all this time did you Rose. She was holding a syringe up. It was pink. This is an anesthetic. That's all that she needs poor thing. I'll give her half and see how that does her. She pushed it in. Maybe her ass her thigh. She stopped. She put her stethoscope down on her heart. She's gone. It was just a bear of her being still. It was all her black and white my father's touchable body. I'll leave you with her

for a few minutes. Take your time. There was a thin young
tech, gay I guessed who dashed out of the room the moment
her heart stopped. He came back & he put a posy orange and
red flowers tiny at her neck. He knows she's Rosie I thought.

He knows the rhyme. It looked so good with her colours, her
enormous mouth going slack. The inside of her mouth was all
out the scar of her lip. Her long jaw. We all cried and hugged.
Do you want to be with her? Yes.

The world was outside the door. It was Saturday morning. It
was so generous. To let us be in here now like this. Just us. She
was a city dog, born on a sidewalk or a roof. There was always
concrete and talk. The world out there now on the other side
of the wall. In here, just us.

How will I ever let go of you girl. The first one ever mine. I
hugged her long body. Her mouth so still. Her eyes, closed I
think. I don't know.

I saw this movie about the jungle. The man died under a tree.
His friends were leaving him. Travel well I said. All the seeds
of you; and the dream of you, the rot.

Then I stepped back into the world.

The Puppets' Talk Show

OSCAR, the host is a puppet. He has shiny black painted hair and bright red dots on both his cheeks. He's wearing a pair of blue overalls with very baggy suspenders and a blue and yellow striped shirt. One of his feet is gone and his pant-leg is empty.

OSCAR: Hello, Hello, Hello, Hello. Our guest tonight, Rosie (a dog!!) is here to set the record straight . . .

ALL PUPPETS: YAYYY!

OSCAR: . . . Yes Rosie is our guest. Thanks for coming, Rose.

ROSIE: (*Nods.*) Glad to be here, Oscar. Very glad, in fact. (*ROSIE leans forward a bit in her chair, adjusting her butt.*)

OSCAR: Puppets, and dogs. A lot of folks probably can't see the connection between our kinds. I say balderdash . . .

ALL PUPPETS: (*Drumming.*)

OSCAR: Our studio audience, the kids . . .

Camera pans to "the kids." Just to the left of OSCAR and ROSIE is a short row of puppets: BEDILIA, who has black yarn hair, MONTGOMERY, a young guy, with painted reddish hair, CASPER (a ghost) little more than a white clown head and a sheet and finally CROCKY, the crocodile. A pair of paper mache jaws going clack clack and a lower body of red and green upholstery material. Behind them are hundreds and thousands of puppets going back endlessly into the horizon which becomes mountains and hills also covered with puppets, all the puppets in the world.

ROSIE: (*Turns and returns to OSCAR smiling.*) Wow.

OSCAR: Yeah there's a lot of us. The meeting of puppets and dogs has been a long time coming and you can see how important it is to our kind. Puppet Nation. No, puppet universe . . . !

ROSIE: I hope I can do my kind justice. I mean there's only one of me—and there's a lot of dogs . . .

OSCAR: What do dogs want, Rosie. I don't mean to put you on the spot. But you agreed to come in today and you can see what your being here means to us. And I hope you don't mind me being honest. You guys are generally considered the enemy. For good reason. Dogs, historically, have torn a good many puppets apart. Tore us to shreds.

Camera close up on OSCAR'S face and tiny tear is dripping down . . .

ROSIE: I get it, Oscar. A lot of wrong has been done. But those do—

OSCAR bows his head then lifts a white hand.

OSCAR: . . . those were ordinary dogs, Rosie. Is that what you were going to say.

OSCAR looks over at his wife BEDILIA and all the puppets up in the hills. He regains his composure . . .

ROSIE: I think I would feel more comfortable on the floor. (*Hops down and plants her head on her paws, looking innocent.*)

OSCAR: Forget it, forget it! You came here to talk with us and . . . it's time to move on. Dogs are pawns and puppets are pawns. Let's face it, puppets are puppets. People put their hands inside us, they enter our heads and our bodies and make us say things whether we believe them or not.

ROSIE: (*Over her shoulder.*) People have us on leashes. People feed us on the floor. They put us to sleep. People put us *down*.

OSCAR: Right, and that doesn't happen to us. But now that you're animated we've got a lot more in common. All it takes to see things fresh is the right opportunity. A good invite. (*OSCAR looks around proudly.*) *To be on our show* . . .

ROSIE: (*Hops back on chair.*) And how many dogs get this, Oscar. How many dogs are called. I'm grateful I was called. I always was. I guess that's why I'm here.

OSCAR: What was it like?

ROSIE: What was what like?

OSCAR: I don't know how to put it. The fame. I mean you're definitely *getting* famous. Right now. You've been written about. Like Lady Di. You're basically being deified. (*Flips through the pages of a galley. Nodding.*) As well as defiled . . .

ROSIE: No great shakes, Oscar. Big dog, little dog. All the same. Humans are the problem. I think you'll agree . . .

OSCAR: (*Nodding.*) *Hmmmm.*

ALL PUPPETS: (*A murmuring begins with OSCAR'S low hum and cascades all the way back up the mountain like a growly bell or a quake.*)

OSCAR: You just touched the rock, my friend.

ROSIE: The one I had rode me like a car. She was interested in *how* she abused me—she wrote about it. She wrote about it extensively. I mean that's why I'm here, right? When I died she described <u>the</u> <u>ways</u> my body was treated: paw pushed in plaster like a criminal or a child—they made a Rosie souvenir before they threw me in the fire—then and only then, and oh yeah and when I was dying, get this, when they're wheeling me around town like a man who has money — then she writes on her long legal pad "puppet, puppetry." She gets the idea that I was used. Treated like I was empty. Great. Yeah well how about my whole long life, Eileen.

OSCAR: That was your name for her.

ROSIE: No it was not. I called her Jethro. That was my name for her and believe me I got in more than one fight defending that name. I tell a few other dogs in the park—ugh here comes Jethro when she's loping towards me with her big smile and a rope like it's good news I've got to go home for hours and sit on the floor. Yet I had a certain amount of loyalty. The dogs in the park got snickering and telling all the other dogs. Look, look, Jethro . . .

I wasn't down for that shit. Laughing at her. That's part of why dogs—dogs in captivity but that's pretty much all dogs—we're known for our loyalty. We stay with the hand we were dealt and we generally will fight for it. Dogs do have choices. Unlike you guys we can move on our own and some dogs totally do. Go to Mexico for instance and live your own life, though you also can fucking starve on those streets. But yeah there's a lot of us down there. I guess anything's better than getting gassed as a pup but—my point was I was very often defending her and getting myself in fights in the dog run *for years* and did she have any idea. First she tries to get me knocked up—had me raped—and that is in the book, to her credit. Later she decides NO . . . THAT THAT'S NOT WHAT I WANT then she has my insides yanked out.

PUPPETS look aghast. ALL PUPPETS.

ROSIE: You didn't know about that. Spaying?

OSCAR: They take your copy thing away. That's it. Isn't it, Rosie. Still, do you want *more dogs*. Isn't that the argument. Alleviating dogs' suffering?

ROSIE: Yes we want more dogs. Do you want more *puppets*. (ROSIE *turns and looks up the mountain and beyond*.) We want to outnumber humans and turn it around. Not in a warlike fashion but gentle, you know. We're doing it from the inside out already. That's what this book means. We are talking to our 'masters.' Very gently and subtly. Dogs are true leaders and strong teachers as the life of Eileen Myles *after* my own life will show. Life is short. That's the problem. It's very hard for one dog to do much in one lifetime. Sixteen years. By the time you hit your message your body's failing . . .

OSCAR: So there's some truth . . .

ROSIE: Truth to what. (*Eyebrows raise*) Hmmph?

OSCAR: Well here's your book. *Afterglow*. It's right on my knee. And what I'm hearing now from you is that it's not <u>so</u> clear how much of the work here is yours. (OSCAR turns towards the camera waving the book.) *Authorship*! Who's writing who.

(*PUPPETS take the cue and start drumming.*)

ROSIE: Want the facts? Ok here's the facts . . .

My lawyer wrote Eileen Myles ten years ago and she did nothing. I was begging her. For years. At least make us some money. The pages my lawyer wrote were brilliant. Can we throw them up on the screen. It's a little long . . .

OSCAR: We're in Puppet Time. Do puppets have time?

ALL PUPPETS: O YEAH! (*Rolling up the mountains and the hills . . .*)

(*Projected on a screen behind OSCAR and ROSIE is the following . . .*)

"*Dear Eileen . . .*"

(*PUPPETS drumming*)

". . . I take the liberty of calling you 'Eileen' to begin the unpleasant duty of forcing you . . ."

ROSIE: (*Off-camera.*) Oscar, have you read this before?

OSCAR: Letter or the book?

ROSIE: Any of it.

OSCAR: I read the whole book. Nothing gets on the show I don't approve of.

ROSIE: Okay so I <u>totally</u> wrote the letter.

OSCAR: What are you saying?

ROSIE: There's no lawyer. There's no money. I . . . I never said it because it kind of confuses things. I put it in her head. It's what we always did. She <u>feels</u> she wrote it.

OSCAR: God there's some legal issues to this.

She must . . . hold on . . .

". . . foundation in their will for . . ."

OSCAR: We've got plenty of time. She must *know*.

ROSIE: She <u>knows</u>. You know how humans are. Particularly this one. <u>Vague</u>. The stuff early on about "the hand-addressed letter" is <u>fiction</u>, just covering her ass. I don't know. Maybe she's trying to give credit to the post office.

But um (*leans forward*) I sent her something else. A dream. It's short. Can I send it to your phone?

OSCAR: Now? (*Awkwardly pulls his large phone out of his overall pocket.*)

EILEEN'S DREAM

At the party I was talking to Peggy . . .

OSCAR: . . . Peggy the dog? The one in Ireland.

ROSIE: No! That's later . . . it's Ahwesh, the filmmaker . . .

**. . . I was talking to Peggy and she
asked me how I'd been. You know it's
very lonely in California but
I'm doing what New Yorkers do
out there. I'm working on myself. I
mean there's no people. There's
people but you don't see them.
Everyone's in their houses.**

**So you can't help seeing yourself. I
went there with a girlfriend you know
and in less than a year she's up in LA**

fucking around. I wind up in a very
large bed, a California king, they call
it . . .

ROSIE: (*Looks down at her own phone, smiling.*) I loved that bed.
Did you get to that part?

OSCAR: . . . Yeah. Let me check on . . .

"*. . . the explicit purpose of identifying dogs who were likely
litigants, candidates for beginning the long and arduous
process of getting the ball rolling on dogs' rights. It's been
clear to my client during her life . . .*"

OSCAR: We're still okay . . .

Eileen cont'd

. . . One night as I was falling asleep
which had been very fitful
that winter, trying to get myself
adjusted to sleeping alone in a giant
bed inside an empty house I began
seeing a slow fading slide show of the
faces of all the women I had ever been
involved with. Each of them was looking
at me with love in their faces, and as I laid
there in my giant bed I found it hard to
believe that that had been my life, that
anyone had ever looked at me that way.

It was a painful lonely feeling and then I
fell asleep. I woke up anxiously in the blue
of morning. I looked out the window
at the eucalyptus trees and felt a stab of
anxiety and realized I must get up. I
jumped out of bed and went into the
front room which had a door which looked
through a tiny yard with a fence out onto
other houses in a suburban street. At
that moment a light went on in the house
across the street. It was the house of a
large depressed lesbian named Junie
who I had determined wanted me by the
way she impulsively grabbed me once at a
meeting. Oh God Junie's going to be
awake now I thought as if by standing
there looking out on the street I was
responsible. I stood in my doorway taking
all of it in when suddenly I <u>saw</u> <u>myself</u>
standing there looking out as a toy, a
wooden puppet with a pointed nose
nodding benignly, smiling and looking
out . . .

OSCAR: (*Lifts his head smiling.*) That's very sweet!

ROSIE: I'm glad you think so. Humans will think it's creepy . . .

OSCAR: Humans NEVER like thinking of themselves as
    puppets. (*Puts white gloved hand on Rosie's paw.*) Your

secret is safe with me. I think we're going live right
NOWWW . . .

*. . . There is one today, the dog formerly known as Rosie. She
has been left a significant sum of money in my client's will.
She may spend it as she pleases with the single stipulation
that she obtain counsel and press charges against her owner
for a variety of abuses and crimes against dog kind. As you
know, Eileen Myles, that owner is you.*

OSCAR: Okay! That's the kind of history we like!! (*He rocks a
little bit, looking at all the other puppets.*)

ROSIE: Powerful document, I agree. And anyone with half a
brain would have written a dog's desiderata on behalf of
us or even a serious defense of herself and we'd be set. No
old Jethro shows it around a bit like look at the brilliant
piece of writing I don't know <u>what</u> to do with and whoosh
slides the letter into her files. Maybe she publishes it in a
student magazine. Years pass. I listen to her whining and
huffing. What's wrong with my life. Why can't anyone
see I'm a genius. On and on. She took me to nature, to
the sea, to the forest. She did her best. When it coincided
with what she considered "her career."

PUPPETS: What's that?

ROSIE: They put their hands inside of you, don't they? Same
idea. Using <u>whatever</u> they've chosen—law, sex, poetry,
whatever they choose . . . they try to do that to the world.

Animate it. Put their hands inside the thing and shake it at the world and wanting everyone to go whoa. That's pretty much how I understand a human career. And we are feathering their beds. So yes I taught her to write. I showed her the way. Work changes in 1990 when I came on the scene. Check it out. She admits it but people think she's being poetic, humble, theoretical. Cut to the end of our so-called story. I'm basically unable to walk to the door to say I need to relieve myself . . . We're sitting on the green chaise lounge in the yard and she's got the yellow pad out and now she's writing to break your heart. Now, you fucking loser. Now? Yes now. The book is here, our book and yes I have helped mightily. Just as I wrote virtually every poem by Eileen Myles from 1990 to 2006 and she wrote nothing <u>nothing</u> in the intervening months, no years. A cat writes a poem. I don't think so. A cat does not have a poem. A cat stays in. It's a whole other kind of thing for them. I'm not really in touch with them yet.

OSCAR: Cats?

ROSIE: Yeah cat. We picked a pretty doggy one. Ernie. Black guy. He was wandering around wondering if this was the right place for him. We took him in and I liked him very much and the pair of them were devastated after my. . . departure. But there's no poems in that.

You know the person you should talk to is Dawn Allen.

OSCAR: Who's that?

ROSIE: She's a talker in betweener.

OSCAR: You mean . . .

ROSIE: Yeah, she's a puppet. She's our puppet. She's practically a saint. People call her up and for a very reasonable rate she lets us speak. Eileen Myles waits till the end of my life to see what I was hanging around for. Was I her father—that's a very big part of this book about me. Humans are always looking for . . . the obvious. Very low, very base, very banal kinds of puppetry. They can't imagine their own animation ending. They decide that god's got his little paw in them. (*Laughing*) I know that sounds a little sleazy . . .

OSCAR: Not to us.

(*Murmuring echoes up the mountains.*)

ROSIE: They decide their children will be their future puppets. They build institutions and write books to carry on their names. Quack, quack, quack. Everything will speak their name while they are alive, and especially when they are gone. The pathetic thing about humans is they think that everything is in their hands, and their hands are in or on everything. Pat, pat, rubbing behind the ears, looking in your eyes for years.

OSCAR: So you had your say. First in the book, through Dawn Allen and now here. I would kill for that experience.

ROSIE: And you *have* in a lot of movies! A doll coming alive, a puppet coming alive. The only thing humans can imagine about puppets finally becoming free of them is that you guys all want to kill. And for good reason.

OSCAR: You said it, Chief.

ROSIE: I told Dawn Allen what I loved. The grass in our yard. The sun on my fur. Jethro was thinking about moving again and in this conversation I let him know very clearly that for me it wouldn't be so good. Dawn asked if I would come along and I used some language that anyone who came from the Myles family should have known meant no.

We'll cross that bridge when we come to it. It was a joke. I was talking like Eileen Myles's mother so she would know in the deepest possible way what was going on.

OSCAR: And did she take the hint. What did she do.

ROSIE: Moved to Los Angeles, of course. She wound up sitting in an apartment in Koreatown writing my will. Thank you! Same old story. Most poets, most humans, for my money, if they have anything going on at all will still prefer singing about it over truly being. I guess it was the best she could do. Poor old Jethro. First she killed her father, she killed the family parakeet and then she killed me

OSCAR: Chilling. Does she know?

ROSIE: She's about to find out. We've written a book, <u>this</u> <u>very</u> <u>sad</u> <u>book</u> about trying to listen. A dog . . . even or especially when our hearing's gone we know what everything means. That the universe is deep. It's not about what's inside of you. The inside is empty.

(*ALL PUPPETS nodding.*)

It's the layered story that is true. That's what everything means to me. The world is waiting. It wants very much to tell you its facts. It wants to be seen. Once you touch everything—and touch it well—then you can let go. And go home.

PUPPETS: You mean?

ROSIE: Then you can sink into the pond and know everything. There's no God. There's no dog! Just water. Everything is water. On and on.

OSCAR: Hah. I think *that* is a very nice place to close.

Goodnight, Sweet Queen

Los Angeles, March 2008

In a couple of days I'll be travelling across America. Just me and Ernie, the king, who daily looks more and more like the old Elvis. A lot has happened since you left. I quit my job and moved. To this apartment in Koreatown I feel like I killed you for. Hope you don't hate me. It really did seem like it was time and I didn't want to hang around and watch you go into kidney failure. I'm not doing much here. LA feels like a giant solarium. You would have liked it. Little more urban than San Diego. I find it hard to think. So I have this low-slung cardboard box of your things I will destroy after I write about them. Some I'll put in storage. I'm looking at your paw impression. Is it horrible. I didn't <u>ask</u> for it. I picture some woman leaning into the wet plaster with you under her left arm. Tight against her breast. That's how I imagine it. Then *whooomp*. Her partner, somebody else, throws you into the fiery furnace. The paw cast could be anyone's. I *prefer* that it's yours. [Clunk.]

PLAID BED (TWO, WITH CAT)

As soon as I situate the fuzzy dog beds on the floor the cat
jumps on them. Ruining the picture. I'm photographing each
thing before I write about it. Inventory is key to the moving
experience. You make a list. I'm assuming you know everything
now cause you're god. Right? The surface of the beds is kind of
"lamby" which made them cozy for you. The plaid along the
trim is subtle like scarves. You were always a masculine girl,
<u>British</u> like an old upper-class dyke. Though you were wild at
heart. My report: I see beige and dark grey almost blue and
of course black. It's plaid like the highlands, like your family's
precious kilt. Plaid is a map of nature, a way of viewing land,
plowed lands, like overhead from a plane when there were
none. Plaids are one of the proofs that we've had extra terrestrial
visitors on this earth. They left us this map. Looking just like
us (no, like dogs) they say this is how your farmlands appear
from our ships. We'd like you to wear it like a flag. To say that
you know. That you won't forget. Dogs look good in plaid.
Always do. Few dog beds are not plaid. LL Bean. The original
dog bed. A dog is looking down from the sky. I'm standing in
a field waving. I'm sorry I let you go.

CONE

Fucking see-through plastic cone. You could've worn this any
number of times. Like after you were attacked by Flora, Jordi's
dog. We came home and there was blood all over the floor and
on your white neck and nobody was saying a word. Betty told

us it happened around the issue of food and we did always feed you guys separately but we forgot to tell Betty. She would never take care of you again. Every dog you ever lived with beat the crap out of you. Hoover biting your neck, nipping at your neck for months. Then at that party you just turned and bit right through his cheek. You were basically very openhearted not that you *liked* sharing your home but there they were. First Hoover, now Flora. I loved Flora, but she wasn't articulate like you. She was a kind beast who enjoyed pears. Which we shared. Last time I saw Flora we were all sitting at Mogador in the outdoor café. You were already gone. I brought Flora a pear and Jordi was so moved but Flora was already eating. How could I forget. We loved pears. How else was there to know, to hold the spot.

humans have dogs

to hold a distant spot close

a star

a cool glow

for the

lonely

BOWL

I'm not so sure what's so special about this bowl. Deep blue with a beige trim. Crumbs stuck in its base. A dab of orange left over from tomato sauce. I always threw my extra sauce over your wet or dried food and because your face was white the orange sauce would stain your maw and you looked stupid plus beautiful. Sauce is makeup around these parts. I also love sauce. I'd let you lick my plate so I wouldn't. I once saw a grown woman, a very intelligent woman lick her plate after dinner. It was a little hard. I liked her so much and it was sort of disgusting and I've thought about it for years. Would I ever be close enough with anyone that I'd lick my plate right then and there? Would I fart? The thing about not growing old with anyone is that you never get a chance to break them in. You'd be all farts right away. Too late, too hard. Much easier to be alone when I'm growing old. I had you.

DRUGS (RIMADYL)

It depressed me when I found the bottle in the cabinet. You'd been taking these tiny white pills for about three years and one time we lost them on the road. Our first trip to CA. No it was our second. August 2002. I think your water bowl fell out at a truck stop and the pills were in it. And without them you were completely in pain all the time. It was unbelievable that these tiny little pills made it so you could bear walking. It was already a total maintenance life but I didn't know. I forgot. You were okay if you didn't have to move but once you needed to pee you had to be picked up and it was the first hint of what the end would look like. Jordi, who we were travelling with, had a cat. The cat's name was Avi. Avi had a tent in the back. Jordi drove a Subaru wagon. We got to the house and Jordi cut a small hole in her office door so only the cat could get in because otherwise you kept racing in and dunking your head in his box. Dogs love cat shit. Who knew? And a pit bull has a very wide grin. Now it was a kitty litter grin. Nooo I'd scream. *I'm sorry* Jordi happily growled as she stood in front of the refrigerator snacking, the door to her office wide open.

After several episodes of feasting from Avi's box you began going to the vet a lot. Maybe she's tired from travelling. She's twelve. Yeah twelve is old. I could never picture you dying but the idea was introduced then. Each new vet would say how old is she. Twelve. Twelve. Hunh. And then look down at her chart. I remember bumping into our favorite vet like the day before you died. I took you to the park on 30th St. that you liked. There was the vet with her friends and it was like she was seeing a ghost. *Is that Rosie!* I can't believe she's still around. I felt betrayed. You spend all this money and you feel so hopeful and then you realize the vet's thinking she'll be dead. Why don't they say let her go. A mechanic would. Get something new, right? *C'mon.* The vet stands there stroking the dog's head. She's okay. You smile. Vet's thinking: she's dead.

A day you could have very easily died we were laying in the sunlight on my bed. This is like 2003. I'm always reading cause I teach and you were lying there. Rosie was. An early fall day in San Diego. Beautiful. And you stirred like you were ready to jump. You stood up and swayed. This tiny sway like I'd never seen before. You hit the floor, stood there a moment wiggling, and with that look in your eye you collapsed. *Someplace* in all of the kitty litter emergencies the vet had said something helpful. Look at her gums. If they're white get her in here quick. Why.

The vet took her stethoscope off. She could have congestive heart failure. So Rosie's lying on the floor and I lift her doggy lip and there it is. Lavender. Pale lavender. I threw her in the Subaru and we drove. Jordi drove and I sat in the back holding your head. Hurry. As the gums grew white.

Did the litter do it I asked. Her spleen had burst. Possibly said the vet. Just keep an eye on her. And we said it together. *Watch the gums.*

I have to say that the cat died too. Avi's now a small agave bush in the yard. I liked him. He was a poet and he's why I got Ernie later on. Jordi confessed that she had once taken care of her uncle's birds in San Francisco and the birds died. *How.* I-I stopped feeding them. I was a kid she screamed in this delighted way. Like she was saying something adorable. First her cat lost fur. Then he stopped eating (which I guess seemed normal since she didn't really eat either) and one night he was under a chair, tiny, and Avi had been a big fat cat and it was like nobody noticed (I mean she kept making vet appointments and breaking them cause she was busy since she was on the job market. I had a job and she didn't. I didn't even want my job and finally *I* took him to the vet but I didn't know anything) so we rushed him to the hospital that night and then he was dead.

There was something bad about my house. In June you began to have fits. Cathy called me. She was a graduate student who became my best friend. She said you were jumping into the truck and suddenly you fell and were lying in the driveway your paws shaking and foam was coming out of your mouth. I flew home and saw that you were weakened but still you were you and you seemed fine. I went back to Toronto and then it happened again. I was back for good.

The fits could happen at any time. I began to be able to feel it same as when you were about to shit. It was like the air changed. I was very wedded to how you were in the world because you held me there with you in the frame. Though I was always waiting. The time I had a dog when I was a kid (Taffy) he was taken away so I only felt safe if I acted like you were someone I was having an affair with and I had to be a little brusque and whenever I came home from a trip you'd be a little miffed and wouldn't look at me but then we'd be on our walk again which was our life. Which felt like my family. We pretended there was no connection which was how we felt it. I vowed now not to ever go away, I couldn't and now the definition was simply us, our intimacy here, and you were dying. I mean all those years with doctors when they asked your age and they *looked*—I mean I knew what they meant but I didn't truly believe it.

They thought *it* had something to do with your white blood cells. They thought maybe it was leukemia. Your heart of course. They gave you tests and put you on that drug and your eyes looked completely crazy. Prednisone. I really hated that drug. I don't like that I said to the vet.

TRAVELLING BOWL ("Outward Hound")

How hard it is for a poet to live daily with a merchant's jokes! Outward hound, ugh! I just finished the first half of Elvis's bio and right as he was having his haircut for the military he said "Hair today, Gone tomorrow." There's a salon in San Diego called Hair Today. San Diego is like the capital of bad names. Every third store name is cute. You feel grateful for Whole Foods because at least you don't have to be offended. You just go in. I'd put your soft blue bowl in my backpack with a bottle of water and a plastic bag and we'd go for our walk. In the later years Ernie followed and a cat friend would follow him. I love how cats follow. They trail and then dart off and then peek from behind things to see where you are now and then never return. I'm finding I'm more of a cat than a dog. Person that is. I really don't think I'll follow you up with anyone.

Yet. I now have around my waist a little dead dog. To think of walking you every day for almost seventeen years. To think of lifting you continually in that last year. Holding your butt up till your rear legs kicked in. Tiny little shaky little sticks. Standing in the piss thinking this is it, the end. I've been in physical therapy (PT to the cognoscenti) for tennis elbow incurred during *any* of the innumerable moves of the past year. Up and down stairs, into my office, up here in LA, all over the state of California. Helping my sister's wife plant their garden in Western Mass. during the summer. But lifting one dog, you, in those last six months was definitely what pulled these tendons the most. You have to succumb to everything. That's what I've learned. I get on a Styrofoam roll and fling my arms forward and back fifteen times a day. I do more and the breath comes back and I feel high and my right arm is getting better. But still I'm carrying that little dead dog. The new fat around my hips and waist is kind of you and how we don't go on our walks anymore. I'm trying

to be different—to do yoga to get over you. I go on walks and
stand on the beach in the forest with no one. It feels sad and I
remain a nervous person. Because when something's gone from
your life it's like the hole a giant rock leaves when it hits a pond
it doesn't just go. It makes ripples and ripples from them and
slowly the circles move out. I've been swaying in this all year. I
know eventually I'll be new without you. But meanwhile I feel
sort of feminized by this loss. I feel fat.

Here's a sad poem I found in the box. I don't think this is really
the title but I enjoy it:

ZIZEK/LOVE/CUB

The inevitability
that God
would be a
man the absence
adding up
to something
and my plants
brownly
scrunching
up to something
cause they
never die
& neither
does my
dog
& neither
do I.

YOUR RAINCOAT

It smells like you. Is this the right place to say that my use of POV, perspective and pronouns is cumulative and historic, performative and not abstract. The raincoat is yellow and reversible. Meaning that I think of writing as a series of presents and the room of the writing is always new. Just as a camera has the capacity to go forward and back, rewind; project or establish depth likewise in writing you have a capacity to address in many ways in the same sentence. Because in fact reality does not occur in sentences and even words are hangers on I believe. Stabs in the dark night and day. We are living in fact in this pulsing film. Your coat smells like you. You are gone and the coat becomes you. Plunked down yellow, rumpled and smelly on a pillow which I stole from the round Holiday Inn in Long Beach I stayed at with Lesley & Jeffrey when we saw "The Ring." It was "The Little Ring." A miniature opera. I love this pillow. Brown with Arabic squiggles on it. I mean a pattern suggesting language though not mine. The background of the pillow is faded. A button dark brown at its center. It's a brown square pillow with a nipple.

So I'm deciding what lives in California and what comes to New York. I think the pillow stays west. The best line I ever wrote is:

I long for a king's progress
from place to private place

A king is always home and that's what I want. And you always had it. We called you Prince Roseberg that fall when you wore the yellow reversible raincoat. Very Provincetown, very beach-y though I don't know that any apparel was ever a hit with you. If it was cold out you were better off staying in. Though you loved the snow. You went wild in it. Dogs don't take showers but their ions change in this other way. I just have to say for once and for all time that you hated puppies. You never saw a puppy you didn't want to kill. And you tried a few times. I was just contacted on MySpace by the owner of one of those puppies. Who was entirely forgiving and then told me he was trans. That's great I said. I don't care about babies either. It's not that I don't like kids. It's just I don't need them and they don't need me. I believe that children are geniuses. And I hope they all have good parents who will let them be. For me it makes a lot more sense to have a dog. Just once in my life. I can imagine a million cats. You will be my dog star always. But a dog star's a double. Isn't that true?

WARNING/SECURITY DOG

I acquired this sign in New York during my presidential campaign. Jane King gave it to me "for Rosie" which I didn't get since you were so kind. Certainly to adults like Jane. Look at this dog with raised maw and jagged killer teeth. The red "Warning" swoops over the dog's head like a collapsed awning while radiating loud noise pain via the dog's mouth. The sign's so punk. It's made out of metal. Jane had a loft and it was the sort of thing a person might have idly leaning against the wall. For several years (1999–2001) I had a loft in New York. Even had my 50th birthday party there. People told me later they thought I owned it. You were at the party of course rolling on everyone who was on the couch. This pit bull is <u>really</u> friendly. The sign wound up hanging on the front gate outside my house in San Diego. Once I discovered you were deaf (and not entirely disenchanted with me) I was afraid you would slip out and never get home. You'd be out there wandering and they would take you to the pound and you would die. Cause you were a pit bull. The sign was a boundary protecting your life. It frightened people so they wouldn't dare open the gate and we were safe.

BLUE HARMONICA ON METAL HOLDER

I kind of tossed this in the box. It reminds me of driving back to California in '05 and giving the harmonica a toot once in a while all the way home and you were in the cab of the truck that whole drive. This time I'm taking a tiny tape recorder and camera. I like this new idea of talking to the road rather than singing about it. Rather than dangerously writing with a pad on my knee I pick up the slim Gumby-like recorder every once in a while. I wrote poetry different ever since the advent of you. I got to follow you with my eyes. Take a step behind, next to and in front of you. We walked to the places you needed to go: parks and beaches. I brought you to the country, to houses to give birth, to multiply. We decided we don't *need* puppies. We've got recording. We were out there in nature and I wrote about you and thought about things in general. I'd leave someone asleep in my bed and take you to a schoolyard in my neighborhood and think about what I had left behind. You were always my boat. You brought me space and peace. I put you in the middle of my life and you never steered me wrong. I got a digital camera in '04. Digital means discontinuous. Discrete. Like a series of 1s, not a whole picture. I liked the recording part the best. When I could pony up the money got myself a handy cam. I took it on our walks. I began a process which I continue today. Little god! On our walks I noted down my thoughts as poetry and then I began filming them making remarks as we strolled. I had such problems with the sound of my voice. Not the recording. The live listening to myself in the sensorium, me here in the world in the park, yammering.

I had this weird experience the year before. We were in the park in the morning and I wanted to write but I had forgotten a pen but I had my phone. I called myself and the text that I spoke was full of pauses. But I was *writing* on the phone. Which isn't the same as what I am talking about but I think similar. I was talking to the world direct and not needing to not forget. And finally really utterly being with you, god.

Which is what I think all this recording (in my life and everyone's) is about. I took a longish walk one day with you when you were so close to your mortality a lip of something you were almost ready to go over and I recollect now that everything all our moments became like that by the time we got to San Diego, our walks became reminiscences of a sort, our present had a pastness to it every day. In San Diego I was so sad. I went there with Jordi which I knew it was a total mistake. She blamed me for giving up her apartment when I said didn't want her coming so I now had to support her in San Diego which was wrong. Then she left me to be in something "more open" in LA.

She put it that way, not me. The poem on the cell phone was about loss. About always flying desperately to another city and being back here now, home. Being in this park with you. And the filmed walks were about the diminishing time we had together. Immediately you were sick and almost died there. When your spleen burst and I spent five thousand bucks to keep you there. And I got sick. I believe that I almost died. My fever shot up to like a hundred and five. I remember saying to Jordi hovering over the bed now what do you want. She said I want to be free. I thought fuck can't you even lie to me when I'm dying.

I took a walk with you once you were gone. I filmed our walk and talked to you like you were there. It's how I've always loved. I wrote some poems about the woman I came there with as if she were still here, when she was already gone. She accused me of being gone. She didn't know what I wanted. You are always gone. I tried to explain to her that what was there was enough. And she was bored with that. My lack of ideas. My lack of desire. I thought I wanted her. She doubted that. Did I? Did I know? Probably not.

I didn't seem to know the difference between when she was there and when she wasn't. It was a fake kind of life, my desire. When I was young, an early teen I pretended to have something in one town and it was how I had it in another. I told all these new kids about the sexy teenage experiences I had in my town and then I went home I told them about the other place. It's how I became alive. My experience made me possible, but it had never existed. My sex was built on sand.

Maybe my love has always been this way, a thing existing in language and so the ghost goes in and out the girl it's based upon and now my dog. I can walk you whether you're here or not. My god! I toss this note into the back of my truck as we drive across the country. I play nothing. I stand up to the mike and talk to you like I'm talking alone, I feel love. I play with the silence now. I squeeze it with my voice: my flow. Driving's so bluesy. And still I can feel you back there in the cab of my truck.

BLUE DISPOSABLE CHUX

Maybe somebody else can use them. I spread them all over the house. Mary across the street gave them to me. Mary lived with Betty. They both used to be in the military and Mary had MS and the US government supplied her with boxes of adult diapers. She didn't use them. You went through at least three boxes. And then I bought some more. I put them at the foot of the bed, on all your dog beds, on the floor. I got expert at layering them, cross-hatching, they protected the furniture. So I did less laundry then and I did a lot. My house was covered in these big blue 'x's. I felt proud. That there was something I could do. That I cared about you. That I had plenty. I had excess. That there was a product. That I had been given a big box of them by a friend. That the government had cared for an ailing dog. That your support came from the government. It made you special, part of the country, like it or not. It was like you were gay. Taxpayers paid for your giant sanitary pads, for your chux.

GREEN DOG COLLAR, STRIPED, WITH TAGS

I bought it cause it was soft. You began to have sores all over
your neck. It chafed. Your neck hair was thin, it looked pink
but that's cause there wasn't so much. A leather collar was
actually punishment and this soft lime green striped faintly
padded one was nicer for you. And buying it gave me pleasure
because I cared. The collar proved I saw things, sometimes,
when other people pointed them out. Maybe Rosie would
like a nice new *soft* collar! *Her neck is covered in sores!* I went
right out and got it. My pride suggests I'm abusive really.
Not heartless but absent like everyone says and I'm saying it
now but you never did. A dog's silence is often construed as
love. After some trip people would say she really loves you.
She acts different when you're around. I'd say really? Cause
honestly I never really knew how much you cared about me.
You liked snow, and rain and air and sun and the beach.
You loved these things and I brought you to them and you
smiled. I suppose I could've imagined you loved me then but
I only knew *I* loved you because I saw you in my way and I
was listening. And you simply were. I loved you for that. For
being who else was in my life no matter what.

The Rape of Rosie

It was a date, it was quite intentional. Though I had never met Buster, Charles had and he insisted he was sweet, not even slightly violent, utterly tan and about five years old. He had the owner's number but he lost it. I'll find it, I'll find it he assured. You will love this dog. And Rosie loves him too. Charles's eyebrows raised. Big grin.

Then there was a girl on sixth street who worked in a store. She was pretty young, early twenties and she knew Buster's owner and she said she would leave a message for him at another store where his friend worked. Then she asked me if Joey another young guy who walks Rosie was my son. That was scary. Or maybe she meant Charles.

Mostly I had given up. Every now and then when I walked Rose some guy would ask me if I wanted to stud her and I always did someday. I collected numbers and put them in my phone book. Tom 549 1694. Sometimes I would write dog next to the name. There's also a few phone numbers in the file where I keep Rosie's health stuff. Usually these dogs look too tough though. Or their owners do. They're the kind of people who ask you to fuck in the street. I want to be tough. I am tough, so I take their numbers. I like it in some weird way. But I never thought of it as the way for Rosie to meet her mate.

Now suddenly she was in heat. I had all the wrong phone numbers and a vacant summer. I kept it free so I could do campaigning[2], but no one invited me to come anywhere till September, and Rosie's two, so this is the time. I was going away for a couple of days and I begged Charles not to let her fuck—I want to watch, but to get their numbers. But I felt sure he would let her get laid and that wasn't so bad either.

Phone rang one night. "Is this the owner of the pit bull that's looking for a stud?" Yes, Yes, Yes, I replied. And what's your dog's name?

We set a date for Friday night. I was sure he wouldn't show. Though she was still pretty puffy (her pussy) I was not convinced that Rosie was still in heat. It seemed so long. Vivien came over. It was pouring rain. Doug lived in Westchester, would be driving down. I couldn't even call this guy direct, had to leave messages on his friend's beeper—who wound up being the guy with the store on sixth street. The date was for around eight or nine. Eight came left. 1/4 of nine. I started calling the beeper. His friend called me back. Far as I know he's on his way. That's what he told me. There was something

2. Eileen Myles's presidential campaign, 1991–92, which will barely be mentioned here.

about two lesbians and a female dog, waiting for this guy and his male that—

Buzz, Buzz, Buzz. They're here. Doug was a blondish guy in his late thirties I think. Kind of American looking. Buster was beautiful. Also kind of a blond, I guess. Should we, we pushed the furniture to the side. It was pouring out. Doug said the roads were flooded coming in. That's why he was late. Everything felt very valuable. I had just gotten cable and we left it on. It added reality to the moment. Were they going to fight.

We were sitting along the sidelines on couches and chairs and Buster would tail Rosie and she would trot away and turn and rear up on her hind legs. She exposed her white chest to him and he licked. She made sweet fighting sounds, growls. Buster barked once or twice. I wondered if I was doing something illegal. Letting dogs have sex in my building. What was normal in this situation? Why did I want that now. It looked like they were going to have a fight. This how they have sex, whispered Vivien. Remember that dog down at the park. Yes, assured Doug. It can be very violent. He's done this before we enquired. Just a few weeks ago. She seems to be quite pregnant. I think you'll be happy with the results. If she's still in heat. She is, he authoritatively assured. Men always say that. The women I know who have dogs make the window of fertility be tiny.

Buster was trying to mount Rosie now. Her response was to sit down. To cover her butt. Uh—oh. Looks like we've got to help her a little. We began to raise her . . . "vulva." We used Doug's word. It seemed so veterinary. If we said pussy it seemed

like we were talking about sex. We would push her little doggy
vulva up with two palms under her butt. She would turn and
try and bite whoever. There were three of us on her now. Do
you have a muzzle Doug asked. It's just like that guy said. Yes,
they can be very violent maters. Oh God, No—well. I tried
calling Delia who used to have Nancy, a very violent pit bull.
Nancy had to be put to sleep. No answer.

You got, you got . . . how about this, I offered. We wrapped
an extra leash around Rosie's jaw. I felt she liked being robbed
of her choice. She stopped trying to bite. I held on, up there.
Doug was positioning Buster. Vivien held Rosie's vulva up.
Doug warned us of not letting Buster get it in the wrong place.
They do that, you know. Buster's dick was pretty huge. I felt
like I was hurting Rosie. What if she's not in heat. Is it in, is
it in. I can't tell. We could use one more person here. How
come Charles didn't come. We got it in. They both seemed to
relax. They simmered. He poked. Slightly. She wavered. Her
whole body wavered. The two swaying slightly together. His
leg cast over her back. She ceased to turn, their two mouths,
their huge jaws slack, hanging open, panting in unison like
big smiles wavering in the night. It was still pouring out. We
all sat down and relaxed—though still holding on. I took off
Rosie's muzzle but held on to her collar. I felt like she needed
me. I had a new experience of my dog's body. She had one.
She was being fucked right in front of me. I felt shame. Regret.
Fear. Excitement.

There was a priest on from Operation Rescue. He was going
on a long theological explanation of the Catholic Church's

deeply thought out position. Rosie's for life, laughed Doug and
I didn't know where I stood. The teevee had a surreal quality
as news came and went, rap groups gazed out to us, enticing
and threatening, the weather continued to be formidable and
the dogs kept at it. It was sex that was impossible to ignore,
yet bureaucratic somehow.

You girls ever hear of Mainstreet USA asked Doug. A shopping network? Nope we replied. From his chair Doug began to
explain his business. Lotta empty hotel rooms, vacations, car
rentals, just stuff. Lot of extra stuff merchants would rather sell
than you know just let sit there. You pay a small fee and you
get this card. He pulled out his wallet and there was his key to
all these purchases. I'm kind of a facilitator. I just got involved
and I think it's a really good thing. I think I can make a lot of
money this way, I haven't yet, but I'm interested so I'm going
to see where it goes. When I meet people I just let them know
I'm involved. They got a video over at the store. Maybe I've
got some stuff in my car. No I think Joe's got it. After we're
finished here, he flourished his hands at the panting dogs, we
can take a walk. Want to. Sure, we chimed.

They had been doing it for forty-five minutes. Is this normal.
Twenty minutes is normal said Doug. They'll stop, he assured.
Are they stuck? We threw the word tumescent around. His
tumescence. She clamps around him. Eventually her water
breaks. That's what it is. And it did. Rosie began to lick her
pussy ferociously when it was over. She looked incredibly sweet
and kind of used. No, spent. That's it. Buster just lied on his
side with this immense pink dick with smears of blood on

it—Rosie's blood. Does a dog have a hymen. I kept thinking of the word tool when I looked at his dick. It was a pink tool. A deep pink. We gave them both a lot of water. They were very thirsty.

Want to go for a walk said Doug. The rain had stopped and the street had that shimmering blackness. Doug had moved out of the East Village a couple of years ago. Couldn't take the filth anymore. The noise, the disgusting people, the attitude's different. I lived here for years. He went on like that all the way down sixth street. Rosie was farting nonstop. What does this mean? We bumped into a buddy of Doug's. Hey he yelled. You know that straight guy yell. People who watch Saturday Night Live. Who stay in to watch it in the seventies. He introduced us to the guy. I really felt like I was in someone else's life. Who are we supposed to be? We were just all having sex. I'm starving muttered Vivien. At the store we met Joe. Everybody was very smiley, shaking hands, but it wasn't about the dogs, it was about the shopping network. He handed us the tape. This is really good. Everyone smiled when we talked about the dogs. The dogs were like these girls we fucked while we were doing business.

Just Before and Just After

If I want for a minute to remember how it felt that summer with my dog, I need only do something ridiculous like go sit in that chair out there, a similar chair like the one I sat in on the floor of the house in San Diego, before the seat tore. I remember the perfect balance of all that just before. The heat in the place was constant, not a wall of heat like the southwest, or an insidious atmosphere of moist sticky heat like it used to be in New York. Not even the hopeless depressing heat of Arlington, Mass. I wasn't even vaguely near the ocean in San Diego but they have one and eventually you could feel it, that shimmering blue body. In San Diego it was hot and you could do something about. And because of the closeness of the ocean an ac seemed foolish. But I could get a fan. I could get us two.

I placed the dark orange sand chair right under the fan and I placed you down next to me with your aged thin summer fur, greasy to my touch, but like living furniture under my drooping hand where I could pat you all day long and read. I was reading some paperbacks from the pile I got at the library sale. And while I'm sitting here let me pass on this small bit of advice to the reader. No one ever wants to hear from anyone at any time anywhere that they have just purchased your book at the library sale. It's like saying hey I plucked your book out from under a forklift just before it was heading to the dump. To write a book is to dig a hole in eternity. It's like after a play you don't go backstage and go: Hey what's new. People do do this. People who don't understand performing, they act like they are at lunch with their friend not understanding that the performer is full of wind and is standing there in the aftermath of something. If you find it impossible to imagine this state then *never go anywhere* near a performer after a show. Not even the week after the show. The performer stands in an insane place on a cliff and if you say hi how are you you are pulling the cliff right out from underneath the person. You're punching Harry Houdini in the gut. People really do that and I'm saying don't.

What do I feel for writers. I feel this. I feel an awe for the incredible permanence of the act of writing. Do you think I had any idea what I was about to write today when I sat down. No I thought I just better do it. And here I am already past the middle of my life. Sitting here humming along on the only road I know. Everything's out there shifting. So maybe the writer should sit still. Like this. In her orange sand chair while the dog is dying. This might be when she would do her writing. People say would you like to come here and read your work. I say no. I have a wind in my heart and I admit it is often eased not just by the act of writing, but money. Yeah. That too. Cause there is also the experience of being seen as a writer, getting chosen, thereby that way getting money. It seems you should obviously always be pleasing somebody with your writing but who. That in part is the problem of the writer.

Truly I live and die like a dog except for the Library. It's what I know. The library is the only true monument to the writer. I think of its bowels warm. So, while I'm not against the kindle, any of the new forms our friend Mr. Booky is travelling in I'm definitely opposed to the glowing screens in libraries that want to lead me to their files, their stacks. I like the card. I like the wooden card file. The collection. I like the ancient smell of the library and its pace. It's home. I can stay in those files for a while. They are the used bookstore inside the library. And all the handwritten information on the card. Black typing, red typing. You could explore. I learned a science fiction writer, Ben Bova, lived in my town. I saw that on a card. "Lives on Lake Street." In the card catalogue I could view the *entire* science fiction category. I could read all of them. I could plunge deep into the sea and burst forth into the heavens (feeling like a god) reeling through outer space for aeons then come home. I'd be the same age but my family would be gone and it would be sad.

My dog reached out. Often Rosie would reach out a paw and place it on my arm. *I know.* I've written myself away somehow. Yet this is what writing is. A leaving behind. A body sits on a dark orange sand chair in San Diego. If I had money I would give it to libraries and you. And all the dogs. Cause you keep protecting me from disintegration and change which is my inevitable home: ash dust and reference.

Maybe they are only selling the paperbacks. That's often what libraries do. Unload all that cheap rotting paper—lousy stock and probably the library has bought you in hard cover too. I'm feeling the breeze created by the fans. I spent thirty-five bucks at the book sale in San Diego. I got a trove. Smelling them. I bought the books that reminded me of my attic room in Arlington, not far from Harvard Square. The hot little airless room I shared with my sister. I read books when I was a kid because I could not sleep. My day had been stolen and I would steal it back now. I may have even been a little tired. But since it was mine to steal, to improve I would slip in another disc for instance one named *Sons of the Ocean Deep*. You didn't have to go to the moon you could go to the sea. The catch to nautical sci-fi though was that we all know about drowning and it was always a possibility.

The science fictions I read when you were dying were neither sad in a real world way or godly. It was just something that might happen next. It was close. And you were down there beside me on the floor, you smelling like corn, sweet old dried corn—rotten skin under fur in the heat and I was turning the mildewed pages of the book. The people in it were walking up roads that used to be highways old broken down ones now, and there were security systems round the houses but somehow the bad people from outside got through and killed a little girl escaping or a man, her father, a brave man died too and the remaining family would have little faith in their own survival. It was just kind of generally about "worse." Everything we knew had broken down after something really horrible happened offstage in the book and now people just like us were going to try but probably fail. There would be big men really thick huge men who changed colors who had no race at all but all races and who would take your soul with their eyes so you couldn't look at them and then his caress would begin a process that had been happening for aeons, like billions of years. One of them or some—he had been fertilizing women with an immensity maybe like Vince Vaughn but even huger. Imagine him Vince Vaughn (always for me a little gross) impregnating across lifetimes not just one man, one bad doctor but impregnating everyone and sometimes pretending to be a woman, say Whoopi Goldberg or Condoleezza Rice. Imagine Condoleezza Rice impregnating many men and women across hundreds of lifetimes thousands of them. For instance one day she just normally goes into the office of the farting president. He looks remote, sad. She's a very smart woman and in this particular life, maybe an Ivy League dyke goes oh Georgie. This is their private talk. A little under it, I guess. They don't like me he says crestfallen while sitting in a pool of his own smelly farts. C'mon. How's about a hug she says. She has said this to him so many times but this one time it is the plan. He himself is turned by the embrace into a serpent female from another galaxy and they are pregnant for thousands of years. It is in him it has always been in him. It was the plan when his mother was husbanded by Aleister Crowley in order to let the serpent female of UX-18 into the human fold. It seems the little squirt was also the hole in the dyke. It is no joke the pun inherent in the lesbian name. A lesbian is actually a kind of punctuation a stoppage in gender in which the characteristics of one kind swirl with the other publickly. A lesbian might be supra female or a lesbian might be quasi man or both. She might be shifting and changing herself. Just to say briefly here the homosexual but particularly the lesbian blatantly reveals the deeper plan inherent in the universe and the resistance to the many levels present in the universe notably often gives rise to violence. Any culture that suppresses the lesbian will die. It is happening now the reformation of the culture because of this crucial embrace, long planned, between the midget president and Vince Vaughn, this mating at last long foretold with the Serpent Queen. Crowley was such a fool. And Pauline Pierce, mother of Barbara Bush an ambitious slut who merely wanted to write her own name large in human history and such people, well all people really don't know things exactly but they nonetheless do see them sometimes and when she mated with Crowley she saw the Serpent Queen of UX-18 (a star you can't imagine how far away—we call it 18—if you laid 18 universes next to each other side by side that would be just one-way—and you've got to return but when you are traveling these kind of distances it is entirely accomplished by mind.) Pauline Pierce saw in the distance as Crowley's forked penis entered her quim she saw the Serpent Queen and she saw behind her a tiny boy sitting in his chair, with a lollipop in his mouth. And she saw an eagle emblem behind him and she was confused and dazzled by this vision. She wrote about it in her diary.

Condoleezza goes gives us a hug. That was their talk. She had said this many times and the tiny boy climbed down from his chair in the president's office and coming up to her he was a man and he needed this size, for broadcasts and cable television and for especially for this one moment (I am sitting in my sand chair in the yard) to have the millennial hug and now everyone and everything in the universe was truly gone or else (we hang thither) just before and just after. Condoleezza Rice was "now" that giant immense oozing man and the tiny president was gone and now one side of the universe for all time (unless something else happens) was impregnated by the other not just for now but for thousands and millions of years and when the child of that union finally comes to term it shall be an army and it will slay whoever is left to fight on the dear old planet earth.

There is a war. There will always be a war but this is the war at the end. Perhaps it is happening now. Pull close.

At this point Rosie my big eyed angel did look up and she . . . yes she did know and she would know even unto the night I saw the possibility of leaving no I would not go flying with you, floating out there in the grey ether surrounding your death and beyond (as if death had a lawn, its spaciousness.)

It's kind of ridiculous placing down my diet coke I said suddenly I stopped patting her. Overhead the fan kept turning. People on this planet are so so enmeshed in their limited understanding of gender when you know. . . the President of the United States who aside from any opinions you might have about his policies . . . the war, and Rosie nodded, and Abu Ghraib—since dogs are the original picture givers and takers of the universe. Children are too but they lose that power—most of them do the rest are unaware of what they've got—they

might use it but they don't <u>know</u> it. Dogs know. That is why
it is so wise to have a dog.

Rosie had been to Abu Ghraib and ever-so-gently nudged the
soldier who took the pictures—first to take them because he
knew in his gut the way they were partying with the prisoners
was wrong and later (nudge nudge) to send them home <u>though</u>
his commander kept making it be known that what happens
in the Grave that was what they called the place what happens
in the Grave stays in the Grave but he sent his pictures to his
mother who worked at the local paper in a very small town in
Gardener, Mass.

Even though the President allowed and was around so much
that we know to be evil, he did seem to be a very ordinary very
essential guy, an American man. Remember the joke about what
he was giving his *wife* for her birthday and he winked lewdly
at the press corps. In that moment you could sure buy in that
it <u>seems</u> we are living in a very dumb almost charmingly frank
men's club—if *anyone* was just a man, our president was, yet
he was a woman of destiny, the Serpent Queen, as promised
in the libraries of all of cellular creation and non-cellular. Is
everything alive you might ask? And a library? Yeah that's a big
question. Is everything a library too?

Yeah and, well, no. Let me answer the first question. What do
you mean by alive? Perhaps I can offer a quote here from a very
famous *female* scientist who put it this way—if every cell in
your body had a vote, you would be in the minority. [Mimes

surprise.] There is no self, no "you." There are many cells, not all are alive, but everything is in play, creating the conditions in which you are living. Now what is your question.

Gender is tiny is the point. Human is tiny. And again Rosie nodded. I ruffle her warm thinning coat. It feels good. Yeah it feels good I growl dad-like. And I am carrying our work out alone. I am writing this up and I must be strong. Yup. I must be brave. I must not forget anything she told me. Yeah. *Pat.* Yeah. *Pat.* Yeah. Beautiful little girl.

I asked my mother once if she thought Rosie was dad. Have I told you this before. My mother's a very spiritual woman. I thought I'll just put it to her.

She said no. I said why. I would <u>know</u>. That was *it*.

My mother is an amazing versatile charming sleeping woman. Maybe it sounds insulting but it's not. You'd have to see her with all her plants and clocks and babies to understand my mother's gentleness. Her greatness. She's very soft. And butch. And she is the greatest storyteller. I think of her as sleeping through her life though you know I'm not entirely trusting the category ("Life.") so my mother might only be walking through a minute in terms of where she's going but in this particular performance I am her lamb, her son, and always I have annoyed her so I am obviously on a journey affecting hers unless . . . well sometimes I suspect my life is what she is dreaming in which case it's good I get some rest in terms of the amount of attention she gives me. I should also qualify her sleeping . . . what it is is a loving—<u>like</u>, rhythm which is steady and warm, a gently rocking boat. You wouldn't try and chat it up. My mother is not bland. She's teeming. She married the man who was my father, an entirely other kind of fellow. If he was a dog he would be the tramp, with a little gay twist. My father did not project a steady sex, or a steady anything at all. But my father saw me and I cannot say on any plane who he was except that after his death he decided to come back again as Rosie because I believe he simply liked me very much.

X³

San Diego, 2005

A dog shakes her way on a leash up a path and now she is gone. We see the empty path with the wiggly hurricane fence coming up on the right and a green clump of bush frogged by lighter green leaves and below it all across in the dirt where paths and slopes meet but it's light. Light meets everything and it's where the color goes. It's what's left when it's gone.

The dog is pooping now and it's rude of us to watch and the dog in the arched all fours of her state, the video is grainy so it's hard to see detail, but we see the troubled look on her face: this is mine, so go away. Her tail uplifted is black, its tip is white.

Out of politeness the camera bounces and soon it is bouncing away. White and tan straw is surging like fireworks. The walk is melting away in the jangling camera work. And soon we're on the path again and a common dark grey rock is as

---

3. Also called transcription, or Rosie at 15.

prominent and seductive as a jewel or a breast. We see dark green bushes then we're at the gate of the park. The dog stands in profile, trees block her head. Her tail's in the air, her shadow falls right next to her. Her entrance, the area is covered in light and the grass bright green almost yellow and all that came before, the bushes and the way have cast an enormous shadow like the path we just left and the past which is always gone.

The dog's sniffy and we take this as an opportunity to look up: the trees of the park and the enormous possibility of day. We're close on the dog, just her legs and her hind parts now. And she's further from us, turning left, her head slightly bowed (with age) her back sloped and she drags her dark leash between her legs. The leash reminds us she is a reckless untrained and impetuous dog who does what she wants. She's freely moving, sniffing and walking slow but it's all one kind of jangle, like a rolling awkward dance and we look up again to see the whole park. The houses and the hills looking down, the tall whitish trees and the explosion of green for smaller ones furthest away so the layered natural world holds us in place. And bars of a playground are over there a way, it's a little unclear which way we'll go. We're trying to decide. More white houses and trees. We examine the park in a circle like this is a crime. Every thing is smoky and dusty which is another thing light does on a hot day when everything appears like mist. It breaks for a moment and the shadows of the trees on the bright green grass look like a spidery hand. Puffy trees bob behind the houses, the complex of telephone poles and wires the houses just arched and arched and now the dog crawls past a couple of skinny trees and dunks her head.

She's found a bit of food. Looks like a big clump of chicken she's eating business-like like old people do; looking up her white face gazing. Suddenly a big mottled tree is jumping around. Flailing we see an aqua painted picnic table and it seems we're high on the delirium of shadows paint pot wildly splashy like dark grey no green like lace all over the grass—tree to grass to tree to grass we're bobbing landing on the innocence of the stone picnic table framed in the valley of sun in the partially shrouded park. This is her throne room and she is either dog or day. We're forced to look at the table again after prowling away for a moment. The older trees are speckled grey a grey brown. And higher up limbs tentacles and the full mushy cascade of leaves and hazy hanging stuff something dead. We go up and up and the browner and bluer and skinnier the tree goes it seems to darken in the pale blue sky. And single strands wave and flare out like well hair or first I thought of cat's stray whiskers the unruly ones but these are heading for the sun. Then there's nothing but blue a box of it and back to the fence. Where's the dog. We're examining the beige real estate behind the chain-link fence, evidently thinking about them and what they've got. Not even a walk. They *live* at the park.

We get her close now. In her animal-print collar. We're right on her dipping head, the rippling muscles behind her ear, the loose hair of the older dog. It's her view: flash of pink tongue and a lot of grass, soon there's only grass a crew cut, and it's black and yellow and white you can see the grade by the sunlight and shadows flashing off-on as she, waving tail and a beige butt and those loopy legs are negotiating an excited run on a good day and she circles the tree itself, rings its color and depth. For a moment you can see the marked slope of her back its weakness but quickly cause why not she's dipping in a female pee an entire existence making the letter, mailman's granddaughter she is.

My Father Came Again as a Dog

My father came again as a dog. The man named Terrence came again in the month of April approximately thirty years after his own death. No joke he came again as dog named Rosie. I titled her so. She came to me as "a tough Irish girl" and I cobbled a name for her according to that assignment. I had been attached to the dog corps for as long as I could remember. Simple liking lead me to the annals of the dog, not the horse. On television a boy with soft hair lived in the country with a furry animal with sharp pointed ears. They had their own show. In another show a gang of city kids had a being along for the ride. One that walked on all fours and a ring around his eye as if to say "seeing is kidding." Look deeper inside. Do as the dog does and the dog does it through taking pictures and sending the pictures around the universe. The team of children and dogs is the strongest link on earth and if we are to survive as a people it shall occur because of the strength of connection in the ranks of these numbers. The future army of the Great War shall be them.

I knew I would be one alone in my family. I was in the middle, the quiet one. The receiver. I felt the tugging from the male side, and another from the female, and those were my siblings. Yet this inbetweenness, this aloneness, hear it now, is holy. I begged my parents fervently for an animal to be an army with me. My story would have moved so much faster if that dog friend had come aboard so early on. If Dog had come into my child life my father would not have needed to return. He knew this and brought me a small sandy dog I named Taffy and yet my mother returned Taffy, this male, to the ASPCA the next morning where he most likely died. His crime? That he had cried through that first long night as all dogs do. I would have learned so much from him. Get this. I would have been a prophet at 12 instead of 60. But I am very grateful to have had Rosie. And her antecedent, the man, my father. And as it stood I was alone in my family, alone in my world, my one ally in the house, the man, my father was dying. I do need to talk about, hear it, the orientation of alcoholism in order to talk about my father. As David Bowie suggested in a powerful film and as certainly Jesus Christ suggested too of the human tribe, we thirst.

There's a very simple reason for the thirst. We are fish. You know the earth was once covered with water and when the higher being who I choose to call Dog felt tired of being alone the waters receded and suddenly there was land. And the fish crawled to land and grew legs. Why wouldn't Dog go into the waters and speak to the fish, in another time, why did the very essence of the fish, some of them, have to change. If you had the powers of a dog who created at least the universe and I have a feeling Dog created many universes but I don't know how many. I am privy to a great deal of knowledge but not all. And this is the very nature of my humility. Even restraining the waters of alcoholism in my own life and I know I know less. And one would assume that Dog could do anything. But no because there are simple laws even Dog needs to obey. You cannot speak underwater. Thus there is no poetry the original speech. Dog wanted to have a conversation with man and the dogs within us. And the fish, frankly, needed to speak. You know how Dog accomplished all this. He pictured it. He pictured an earth covered with water and he pictured it dry, listen to me, and the fish going up on shore and discovering feet. Dog is lonely, we can see that "lonely" in every dog's eyes and that loneliness is love. It causes us to do good things. Hear this. Such is the power of our army. Because the enemy of that love is dying. Every dog is fading slow returning to the waters of time which is the nature of dog's eyes. His seeing is the sea.

Meanwhile on this earth on this planet we are thirsty. Are we brave enough to see this thirst as longing. We want to go home. So we go to the beach. Understand! We wait for night. The little living human is framed, is continually, by opposites. One of the ways we experience this in the living realm is in the limitations of things. Can we accept this longing, feel it, even maybe occasionally go down to the beach. Jump in, dry off and walk on. Do we accept our fate? The holiest people live by the sea with their dogs. Look at Mary Oliver. That is a saint. But there are a great many challenges to our frame.

Think of a mind as a sea. Its own inland sea. We can connect to the enormity of others, the sea in them. We can connect to Dog. Hound of the Ocean as the ancients once said. But there is an agony at first but maybe a little all the time. A kind of oceanic stretch. Aching, impossible thoughts. Some people take a giant leap themselves by being "gay." Other people need to kill them. Cannot accept the thought, the "gay" thought. That things are not as solid as they seem. So there are many sudden inexplicable deaths. How can we abide. There is a sea. There is Dog. Can we trust in that deep silent underwater bark? The ripples allowing a stretching of thought, a wide lookage. To be living in that lighthouse. Thoreau knew it, wrote about it. Yup, you know him. Hear this. To be standing in that light. All that light. Because every day as we are dying our gaze is getting tiny without Dog. We become sorrowful. We can cry out. Wait for this now! And hear her sorrowful knowing bark. For Dog will come to comfort us. We can do evil. Be violent. Use love as if it were a common bone lying on the ground. An inscrutable bone. Using it there. Yes.

The only true logic is sound. If you don't know, listen. Bend yours. Careful here. An angry murmuring, an ill placed yelp, a grrr can set off a maelstrom of pain, tragedy and disease. We need to get it right. To listen well. To not do wrong. We need to abandon our logic and go back. To wait in dog is to get on all fours, not just on your knees, but to worship the dog privately and wait. The waters are coming, we can and we will replace the violence with silence and wait. The peace of the dog is promised and soon will be upon us. His waters will rock us and hold us. He is the sleep. He is the night.

But normally humans want to drink. I'm a little parched they might say. How about a couple of brewskies? Some smart drinks say the lifted eyebrows under a spectacled gaze. One eye shifts towards another in an office. A tipping gesture like a drink to the lips is made. Glasses into purse. Computer turned off. Okay? There is so much surrounding this urge to drink. A young person might feel, uh, a powerful tugging in their crotch might begin. A thudding inside it is the sea of desire to which all are privy. And all around the youth the message is no. What you feel is wrong. But it is inside me. This is what she says. This is what he says. Is this feeling not right? The youth drinks and the conflict is resolved. The illusion of alcohol is that we are putting the ocean inside. But no get this. Instead we are stilling it. We are dying. Alcohol is mold. Past ripe, a sickly sweetness that makes a person go crazy. Of beer they say the kiss of the hops but it is the hiss of the snake. The snake laughing uproariously whenever a horny teenager takes a drink. Her head cast back in exaltation, her hand fluttering at her chest. She is the antithesis of dog, the agent of counterfeit sweetness that is replete with a message of death not life. SSSSSSSSST. It is not the healthy surf pounding against the rock. Another picture: the balloon of your soul deflating.

When two people meet and engage in the act of fertilization simultaneously a million pictures are surging in their brains. Think of your parents making love if you will. Pay attention. An academy award, a cavalcade of thoughts of pictures is coursing through their heads. Yes, right up here. You are one of them. The universe is a tiny yearbook but told in seconds. The possible second of each of us. I must explain here for the first time perhaps that the act of sex is not the sex act as we understand it. Oh no. The tiny picture is key instead, a thought entirely understandable to children who intuit pro-creation entirely. They are for it, standing at their drawing pads in kindergarten. Don't get the wrong idea. The collusion of childhood and sex in our time is the greatest of crimes because we are wiping out their supreme board by imposing too early animal sexuality on a greater moment. I am saying the child is a virtual movie theater, get this, not of sex but of creation. Get this. True creation. The first eight or ten years of the child's existence are full of these pictures. The supreme board, listen here, your light bubbling portrait gallery, the cattle call of images from which all of us were chosen, this is the wild field of life. People in their natural state are sometimes unable to make a selection. You know how the drunkest people often have children. Easily. While the earnest twos, good people can be plugging away at it for years. Even the lesbians trying. Good people too! It is enormous the responsibility. Which is forgotten after the act always. I tell you now. The two of them engaged in the act must see you momentarily—you are the thought. They must go: Yes, *her*. Few can sail into this mode of selection readily. It's a trance, really. Sex is given humans to distract them from a lighter deeper choosing. That is a fact. It is easy, a child could do it, pick a face, a nature they like from the sea of entities ready to be born. But the world already is terribly crowded. The child must pass a few years; this is the waiting time. The true gestation. Later on they may enter into the deep rich valley of sex: the place where the human first encounters the nature of soul. And it is there at last that our widest choosing has begun—as we begin absently putting our arms around vagrants, elves and villains, around thinkers, teachers, pilgrims and beasts—in this rambling sex time and the map of creation is streaming through our heads all the time here on earth hear this it is *manifested* by the fitting of bodies, one to another. It is a holy place, not a holy act. Like universes if you see where I am going. I have given you many talks. This is one. The greatest crime on the earth of course is rape. Animals commit this crime as well. Dolphins and ducks. The spider many times . . . she then eats the perpetrator of the crime. I am not saying the spider's way is useful for us. Rape is . . . prepare for this thought. It's stealing the envelope of another. Bodies, though gorgeous, are only containers of the sea. If you force your way into a message that is not intended for you, it's a kind of suicide. The message will annihilate you ultimately. You're no one now. On and on. You are no one for generations if you do it repeatedly. It's very hard for us to understand it on this plane. The greater suffering is endured by the one who has forced their sex on another. Holy people have said this about their torturers too. It is very hard to think about rape this way but it is true. That there are no pictures. If a child is born of this union they either have no mind or they are sage. There is nothing written on these minds and either nothing good will come of these people or they are the saviors of our time. In the future I see a small yellow dog in this position. And he is the prophet and he shall be the end of this story. For today I see my own teacher, Rosie.

XX

She smiles because she's happy galloping off slack jaw and the slopes of the park are a sea variety enabling her watery legs to dance with her rear legs getting a pass as the front does all the work and her ears in the air.

News of the dog: here's the fence again, and a willow tree probably Australian. There's a tall blue and red plastic ride we fall into the shady bowl of it a sec. Aqua bench. Can a park be childless. Teen markings be all that signal we're on earth. And up the tree into new bright green leaves: birds are singing and the dog is only ass, her forefront dipped entirely into the bushes. She knows the score. Cause she's *old*. She can eat whatever she wants now. Shit, chicken bones it's hers. In fact she may choose her death. Did she.

Deeper in and she's gone. So we find on the other side her white maw thoughtfully munching a muffin or a leaf. She turns around her tongue hanging out her white face blazing and this is pure joy. She is fifteen. The sun highlights all the wrinkles in her barrel chest. A soft torso that used to be strong but the

width and the heroic bone structure, ripples and inclines now
say where the muscles were. She doesn't care. She wears her
body like her favorite clothes. Age is a slight inconvenience on
her way to sudden meals. Her paws and lower legs are white &
the upper is a splash of honey. Above is pink: inflamed, puffy,
raw the sores like the exposed torn joints of a stuffed bear.
Watching you is so much yoga. Each new attraction makes
your head drop & turn & we see the white under maw which
I used to call "velvet" when you were a pup and now I call sort
of wash cloth.

There's moments when all I can do (and I can't) (and I did)
is rub my palms along the shifting grade of your butt, back,
shoulders. It's a bit of a slide. She's moving in wood chips round
a disc of hot cement. It's dancer-like: late "Merce", each paw
falls deliberately and ripples with the rest. She snakes. In a way
only her tail is testament to how uneven it all is, tadpole to
the highly erratic path of her walk. She lowers her head to the
base of a slender tree and the silvery bone flickers madly from
her neck, her only jewelry, ID.

As if we're in another world the sidewalk suddenly is cool blue
and yet she's totally turning to the right, she's walking away.
She looks like she's going into a restaurant she practically owns,
she's that kind of man.

Moments are speechless to arrive in a patch of grass shaped by
cement on the other side two sworls and they contain grass wood
chips sun and pit bull that's what it has. It's very still. Holding
these events from seven or eight years ago even making a screen

shot of some like a lonely applause.[4] A bird chimes in knowing. And there's the *here*. A world of traffic outside my hotel. I can *peel* up the corner of the walk. This is a risk. And I hear the rain of another country, another century. Not that grand. Pouring rain. It's really pouring here, no there . . . no ecce.

She's huge now close. We're at her back. The physiognomy of dearness unsurpassed. Neck and shoulders soft wide, held up by the bent flagging legs its own form wiggled in dark echo tall taller to its right. We let just shadow walk for a while. No dog only its repetition. Sentimental painting last Indian on a cliff. Then two dogs the shadow dog and the white, the white and black and tan are feeding on something making an eight of legs, a thing and the tail arches to say it's time waving. She dips and pees and turns around. *Okay* she says impatiently tired blazing and yet.

There's a tree that's mostly dark. I stand next to it. Enormous legs now enormous dog. The folds on the inside of one chicken bone leg a part of meat of calcified muscle, a folding a friend. The dandruff in her fur, her skin is flaking. The tub of her, the tube of her—intelligence lifted and gazing. Motto: *Always aim before moving.* Into the same wide procession of green, turning, going. Only two feet left. And we can feel the grass now with our own paw.

Back into the brightness and you're still walking a friend, the other dog, and the world is staggering now bouncing

---

4. Screenshot produces grey geometric pattern. That's not Rosie.

complicated green and suddenly your limbs are blurry and close. And it's simply traffic the exchange of public lawn and dog on and on for a while and we can think our thoughts.

Dirt feels different. I'll say that. It's *dirt*, a lemon squished and the detritus of willow, a smattering of strands. We hold onto the squished lemon half cause the color is wild and we need that. Cause it's only green and doglegs entering for a moment. Shaking the jar. She definitely wants to go home. She's shade and dog. Dark posed one thing before the dark concrete and fence bright reflectively in the sun. We're done. And smells home half way through and stops.

And it's that house, the first one. It looks like a tree: yeah tree but it resolves into dog small fuzzy dog beneath a messy grove before a beige house. Freeze it.

Go across the room and sitting on the toilet to look at this worship. Such a long reminiscence. And I'm the dog. Luminous somehow. In the room, outside, on the screen. Just a glow of light on gravel.

Peel.

She turns a blazing, thirsty white-faced tongue out member of the dead heading home. White stripe of sun on her back. Across the silence I'm calling. *I'm your man.* She turns and looks back holding still. And she moves which means come. Come with your dumb camera.

The scratchy swirl of beige you can't not notate. Grass. And now her head peeks in like marginalia.

I get it. The *corgi* is here. Younger with an upright curious sympathetic face. The older dog endures. Stands in grass. She jumps and it's her chubby legs we're locked on. Two dogs circling limbs in green grass. I thought we were going home. Everything's between the lines. Where did this corgi come from.

My dog's getting petted by a man. You see the pile of loose hair on her back. You can see his pointed loafers now. His tumbled jeans. And the corgi is running around circling Rose.

And Rosie jumps. She always has energy for love. The man touches her shoulders. Her neck. He brushes the hair off. The corgi runs around. Then Rosie looks up. Right into the eye of the camera. The unambivalent fact. *I thought we were done.*

What is that. A pole? A leash. Just human legs a shadow walking across the grass. Tiny dog mid-field. Oh yes we're coming home. Face close up. Weary. It's me that's weary. Of copying, of writing, of filming. Of killing my dog.

She's nothing but a blur. I hold the insubstantial joy like a child. And now my head is out and her face is out. I give her a grey brown treat. A liver square and she engulfs it softly off my hand and I feel the wetness that accompanies the act. I get a lick.

FOAM[5]

Hello! I was hoping to start this talk with a recording of foam. Is Juliana Snapper here. I don't see her . . .

Okay. Well let me begin. In 2002 when I taught at the University of California in San Diego I had a student named Tristan Wand and he was a surfer. Whole school was. Flip flop U. Boards hanging out of the back of their cars. Tristan was writing his senior thesis on La Jolla's past—there was like this guy underbelly he wanted to write about. It had to do with these dudes up here in the '60s, the pump house gang they're called in Tom Wolfe's book of the same name. Guys crashing cars, being outsider in a way that was a little unclassifiable—then and probably always—into surfing and getting wrecked and of course La Jolla today doesn't have any of this—being sort of Palm Beachy or East Hampton. But Tristan worked at a

---

5. I gave this talk at the San Diego Women's Center in 2007. Then I wedged myself onto a panel about Hyper-objects at the Eco-poetics conference in Berkeley (2013). Timothy Morton was our chair but he didn't show. Probably my fault. Then in April of 2015 Jennifer Firestone invites me to give a talk at the New School on Feminism, Pedagogy & Writing. I gave it there, I give it here. EM

restaurant with those guys from that generation, men replace-
able with one another, a string of them like a line a chorus line
manning the kitchen at work, do-nothing dads, my age, who
got wrecked last night and so one might not show up today but
the other one did and they had a constant laughing mumble
among themselves as they stood in the kitchen doing work.
They scared and fascinated Tristan while he stood among them
and I suppose he didn't want to be like these dad surfer guys
and that got him into the idea of writing his senior thesis about
them. I was his advisor and while he was telling me about the
guys I drew this:

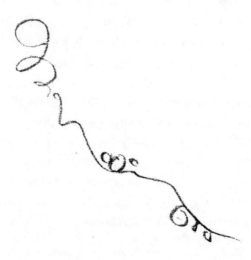

I was imagining his guys like a chorus of bubbles not separate from each other but a string of things of words. Not in the ocean, but not far, kind of a strand, like the tiny string of bubbles on the beach when the tide has departed, that strand. Look I told him, or maybe he did this drawing and gave it to me. It's a squiggle, not much.

Use that. It's abstract, don't you think. <u>Keep</u> <u>returning</u> <u>to</u> <u>it</u>. That was my advice. What it all gets reduced to somehow. And quietly I thought I will also do something with it in the time I'm stuck here which turned out to be five years . . . those guys, their wasted lives, so beautiful, but what.

I woke up early today. Figured I'd just keep working on this talk long as I can. I brought things here, to this beach town, a gorgeous fertile animal (when I say fertile I mean like generative) and I also took things back with me. Writing (it is my belief) is sort of a performance and text and ideas and bubbles are always frothing & coming right until the last minute. Foam is kind of a radio show.

Robert said please don't be academic. I'm not. What you do in the bum-squat institution is your own thing but I taught a class here called Pathetic Literature. It began with a form of masculinity. Here. Look at this picture I have of myself stealing a nickel from a bank. I am about nine. I look exactly like a boy but it was a long time ago. I orchestrated the photo so I could be apprehended as a bad boy, a thief. Gender could <u>be</u> I guess just getting *caught*.

In the art world in the eighties & nineties pathetic masculinity was a bunch of guys doing fuzzy work. I mean soft and cuddly and a little unclear. Men knitting, making crafts. I even think of Beck. & god rest his soul Mike Kelley. It was hot stuff— loser work these guys were doing. Talking about their feelings. Definitely they were tucking their genitals a bit. They were also dropping couches on their moms and making pornographic elves. Which I get! Elves are hot. But here's the thing. The secret about the pathetic men is that *they had all studied with feminists.*

Look at the shows that are around right now—in LA, in New York. One in Spain. Everyone's looking at women. It's *big*. [Look down.] Great. My foam just rang. Ha-ha. Julie's not coming. Great. But [puts phone away] this guy, the scientist Julie told me about is recording melting. *Sound* tells us how fast global warming is occurring. I once called a glacier and heard it speak. No that's true. You'll find it in *Iceland* not to uh utterly reference my own work. The structure of crystals is not unlike the structure of foam. I'm talking in a women's thing today. Right and today millions of women are rising up all over the world in light of the violence against them. The feminist shows I think are in light of war. Didn't we just attack Iraq for no good reason. The Brooklyn Museum in response bought Judy Chicago's dinner party. So fucked up! [Slam hand.] Other museums had similar shows. To create the illusion of an economy. I don't think it worked. But here's what women artists did. They were measuring. They were recording the family as part of *the science of feminism*. This is serious. This is what they did in the sixties seventies and eighties. Mary Kelley creates a <u>chart</u> of her baby crying on graph paper. Eleanor Antin does one about the in-laws coming over. Go right to the museum and see it. It's like personal art gone conceptual or vice versa. *Because* the feminist artists understood the radical ironies of living in the 20th c. more than anyone else *because* they were women and had not ever been <u>fully</u> <u>breathed</u> into the economy. In the pathetic course at UCSD (I sprinkle it here) I simply taught that those guys studied with these women. The gay ones even having dances for themselves with long velvety banners and making cushions with things on them about dyke love. They were making craft stuff in the seventies and eighties not like PTSD World War II dads making bird houses in the garage (well exactly the same.) These ladies no their collectivity was something <u>monumental</u> that floated rage and was *for* sexual freedom and also made jokes. Problem still was they were women. The art world had to wait twenty years for the guys to come along and paint *their* diaries large on the walls of major museums and write about their personal lives and make bad cartoons and knit bunnies. The concept is clear when a man does it because a man has to DO SOMETHING in order to be pathetic. He is not intrinsically pathetic like a woman is.

Mike Kelley actually said in an interview around 2004 that despite people always asking him about feminism and its affects on him it was really beside the point because when he does craft he is being IRONIC whereas when a woman does it she is being natural. I don't think these women knew that. Which is the difference between a woman and a man. A woman may think she knows something but in time history will see that she is just being a natural woman whereas if man means something, *it stays*. There's a monument to men, that's what the world is.

Okay. I'm still thinking about the books we read in class. *Dialogues in Paradise* by Can Xue has a woman who had an awful mother. A horrible ranting woman. Makes you jump a bit? I like that. A woman so bad her own daughter had to leave the room. There was a bucket of water in the room and when the daughter returned her mother was gone and there were just some dirty bubbles on the surface of the water. And dirty clothes next to the bucket. The mother was gone yet her cruel complaining words were still bursting out from under the water. Bah Bah Bah. Complaining and making life miserable for people. The horrible speech kept ascending and falling back into the slimy bucket. It was beautiful. She was melting, becoming less. In the end the mother was just this slimy residue. Of sound?

There was foam all over the books I assigned. No one was fol-lowing it but me. Foam again I'd shout. It was not the thing the class was about. This slime on the side saying something. My plan for today's talk was to go back and re-read those books and see what the foam was all about. Valerie Solanas. Robert Walser. Samuel Delany. Laurie Weeks. Dodie Bellamy. Kevin Killian. Deleuze. All frothy spitters and droolers. The books among other things were about gender. Because gender *makes* excess especially when it's unstable which it always is. It's pathetic. It has some extra stuff and it expresses itself in nature in these tiny bubbles on the sides of trees. Speech coagulated or blasting from the corners of your mouth. Balloons rising from the cartoon heads. Talking, yeah, but what about *thinking*.

That's where bubbles come in. It's pretty quiet in here right now but I know that you're thinking. Like to take responsibility for those thoughts. [Opens can of diet coke with a loud pop.]

OK there's just something hopelessly queer about foam. Last night I found these things about buildings in China:

The Water Cube employs water as a structural and thematic "leitmotiv" with the square, the primal shape of the house in Chinese tradition and mythology. The structure of the water cube is based on a unique, lightweight construction derived from the structure of water in the state of aggregation of *foam* [my emphasis] deduced by Weiare and Phelan of Trinity College, Dublin.

Behind the apparently random appearance hides a strict geometry found in natural systems such as crystals, cells and molecular structures. By applying *novel* materials and technology, the transparency and randomness is transposed into the inner and outer okay *blah blah blah* . . . Conceptually the square box and the interior spaces are carved out of an undefined cluster of foam bubbles, symbolizing *a condition of nature that is transformed into a condition of culture.*

I don't think there's a wrong place to turn here, do you? So marvelous. One of these descriptions of foam architecture actually talked about the *yin and the yang* the implicitly masculine and feminine aspects of these kinds of structures. And of course sea foam.

In Greek mythology, Aphrodite is the goddess of love, beauty and sexual rapture. According to Hesiod, she was born when Uranus (the father of the gods) was castrated by his son Cronus. Cronus threw the severed genitals into the ocean which began to churn and foam about them. From the *aphros* (sea foam) arose Aphrodite, and the sea carried her to either Cyprus or Cythera . . .

When I told Jocelyn Saidenberg about this she informed me that Cronus in fact castrated his father because he <u>could</u> <u>not</u> <u>bear</u> the spectacle of watching his mother Gaia be incessantly raped. That is so amazing to me. I have always hated Ovid because it is just rape. I hate reading myths. I liked them when I was a kid because I didn't know what sex I was. And I hate history. Iceland is essentially populated by the descendants of raped women. Probably all of us are, right.

When I moved to New York in the mid 70s my roommate showed me a lesbian poetry magazine called *Aphra*. I kept throwing my stuff at them and got rejected again and again. I didn't even like the poems in that magazine. I didn't know it mattered. I didn't know about liking yet. The journal ran for only eight issues. *I* think it's because they named it wrong. Because *aphra* means dust. To be fair, a snowflake is dust with a little activity going on. Yet foam (*aphros*) is code for a deeper knowing. Like magazines. And even books are not about the work, but an experience or a place. I can already imagine you getting mad when you hear this. Good! My purpose is this.

Aphroi (Africans): Name of a people; the Karthaginians. [They are descended] from Aphros who was king of Libye, the son of Kronos by Philyra.

See the information's a little buried here. I'm reading it to Joan (Larkin) and she says *that* makes sense because supposedly Africa was "the middle of the world." The birthplace of the human race. You okay?

April is first recorded in English in 1297, as "aueril." It comes from Old French "avrill," which is from Latin (mensis) Aprilis "(month) (mons) of Venus," the second month of the ancient Roman calendar, dedicated to the goddess Venus.

The Roman goddess had many names, as she absorbed different regional and cultic fertility goddesses in Italy. The name used for this month [the one we're in!] is perhaps based on Apru, an Etruscan borrowing of Greek Aphrodite, the Greek goddess of love and beauty. Her Greek name traditionally is derived from *aphros* "foam," from the story of her birth, but perhaps it is ultimately from Phoenician Ashtaroth (Assyrian Ishtar).

Let me give you this one little bit of finale:

Aphrodite's counterpart in ancient Roman mythology, Venus, was the goddess of beauty and love, especially sensual love, and Venus in Latin literally means "love, sexual desire, loveliness, beauty, charm." The reconstructed Proto-Indo-European base of this is wen—W-E-N—"to strive after, wish, desire, be satisfied."

I feel like this talk is a libretto. It's not <u>here</u>. You know what I'm saying . . .

My point? *Foam means I want.* Is it the trail of it, the tingling stuff on the side as I'm reaching. Cunty, even? Waters churning when they pitched the severed genitals in. Like cooking right. Not that I cook.

Joan, it's like magic. The woman stirring the pot is *a witch.* The woman's place in the kitchen is like . . . a castrated form of magic.

Eileen I think cooking is powerful stuff. Joan's a good cook. Okay but . . . don't you love the idea of a dick and balls whatever Cronus cut off his father becoming an *ingredient,* like mandrake root, lizard foot rather than a grand force, just another item in the soup. Throw it in. [*Splash.*]

Stir, stir. Well that's good said Joan. I like ingredients, she said.

I think foam also looks like pubic hair. Sort of curly. Waves, like design. In church, I thought. This is from 1960 or '61. I'm with the Delays, Patty and Ruthy. We're in a pool in my backyard and my mother had thrown some soap flakes in with us so we are playing in foam. I guess when mothers see kids in water they immediately got cooking turning play into a bath but we turned soap into hair. Did *you* do that—you know draping soap bubbles under our arms, on our chins and side-burns and laughing when my mother went upstairs—between our legs. Make a big hairy ass Patty urged as Ruthy obligingly got on all fours. The future was a joke and we told it in soap.

But how did we know about all that hair, our sex, what did we feel. Did we know hair falls out when you're old. How do *I* feel about this. And you stay clean longer. The soap goes the hair goes everything. They wash your body when you're dead. The foam dries between your legs and nobody cares. Doesn't even feel bad.

Look at these little wands I have. Like letters. Bubbles on a stick.

Joan reminded me of soap pipes. This is in the forties and fifties. You would have a pipe and your mother would supply you with a bowl of soapy water and you filled your pipe and sat at a table blowing bubbles out of it, streams of soap bubbles pouring down. Not hair but smoke, that was the sign of the adult. Pouring out of their nostrils, drifting from their hands as they spoke. Lighting up when they got together. Sharing a light. Got a match. Think of the magic of that intimate sharing. The bending, cupping and smiling. Cigarettes in bed. On the plane. Opening the jacket. Now the smokers are all outside. Shall we join them?

My dream is that history is backwards. What if I'm born of him, Cronus—of his anger and his drunkenness and the ripe destruction of his father's weapons. I'm for it. And I know these men.

This myth might take the story back. When I was a little kid we went to a beach called Stage Fort Park in Gloucester just like on over-cast days. It was foggy and I was always dreaming of my little men. I feel I was born there. The beach was a dream all covered in fat brown seaweed and these rubber balls I thought grew naturally there and I feel I could almost hear my boyfriends wandering and whispering. Blinking and vanishing. My family was always in such a rush. We didn't have time. Can we go back there and find him. He has to be there. I keep looking in the spray and mist for him, my son.

XXX

We're sniffing in front of the techno house that has fights and Ernie jet black Ernie is there. *Who* pissed here. It's later in the day and the shadows are covering the street. The neighbor says hello but I think she's monitoring us. She laughs cause the cat's taking a walk with us yeah I actually make her laugh in that friendly way. I say something and she dangles her baby out the door so I can take her picture too.

We examine the glories of a very distressed yellow fireplug marked with the tell tale "R." Not graffiti. That's fire department. Meanwhile the gentle tap tap tap of the music of the house still pouring out. One side of the fireplug is blue. Chalk blue. I want to say scrawl. The cat seems to get distracted so I'm luring him in. He looks back at this day. More agitated it holds a white dog barking jumping up and down. The wall behind him is rose faded salmon in sunlight going to white. Blazing. My yard he barks. My sidewalk. We're close up and all we see is whiteness and fence. The entwined genius of chain-link fence. Leg's barking a brindle head staring. Is it two dogs. I see anger & long stuffed yearning. These dogs are fucked.

Finally Rosie leading with her head. Fences covered in dried vines strings of green leaves. Rose says (sniffing) *covered in piss*. Her fur has thinned one black stripe gleaming in the sun as it fades to the sides. She's clean as hell she's bathed a lot because of her skin. Here's another dog. Poodle I think, white. Each dog animates a yard: I'm here and what the fuck do you think *I'm* doing. Everyone's "in" when they'd rather be out—they're in-out in their kingdom. This is *all ours* me and Rose. Cause of this ritual, our walk. Because of the camera. I remember when they built that strange web of supportive stone beneath this fence. Really fucking ugly. It's the fashion here. To r-a-i-s-e the yard. I think of the violent husband I met one day yes this is the violent reward. Beauty just a big apology. This dog's got button nose button eyes lifts his head to show chin but mostly he stares. This dog wants to play. I am locked in my position attached to you and you continue to sniff. Now a baby squeals, dogs barking and across the street on a low wall of brick lions. We look across the street and back. Bark bark bark. Thank god there you go with your sandy back. Oh and now an empty bag of Lay's. I'm trying to duplicate what the dog sees like ecstasy but it's not. There's a small purple flower the sweetest thing with its folds and its brighter pinker twin you look *in* the flower and it's paler I can't just go white but the flower does. A silent blaring horn. Finally you head with the white dab onto the screen. Into the square. We walk along a row of leaves chewed on by bugs purple flowers cars telephone poles trees this is California. Little luxuriant a little condemned. O look what we did. When all this was canyons and wild. Only blue. That god. Wand of the telephone pole reaching beyond makes this blue square active. Wad of me walking and you. Head and shoulders. Little mayor with your neck and head covered in light now and we turn onto a street that is dirt.

The Navel

Women above all should not drink. Gender is an untrustworthy system and at the deepest point its waters are pure myth. If you could see the supreme board of all of mankind unfortunately these records are being updated really wish I could show you but I can't. Trust me that where each of us is checked off as M [ ] or F [ ] that column is blank. Well what am *I* you're asking. Blank. That's what I said. My father? Blank. My lover? *My mother?* Blank. Gender is a place you have parked your car one day and one day only. That day is your life. And in that spot a mother's inattention opens directly onto the Chora[6] space which is everything, the source of language for example so in every instance we urge females not to drink because with each sip they are destroying the language which will happen soon enough. I do not mean no drinking so that they will not be raped. They will be raped. The females will always be raped. The tablets have been smashed, and they will be smashed again.

---

6. The Chora space is a church in Istanbul dedicated to the Virgin which has a navel on its floor the navel being connected to heaven. During one of the takeovers of Constantinople an infamous whore was placed on the throne to desecrate the church but really she just stirred what was already in there. Legend has it she wrote poems sitting on that throne.

We are keeping no secrets but holding back only temporalities. And as to whether you are this or that (I mean gender) obviously there is no need to keep records of that tiny insignificance.

I said earlier that if every cell in your body had a vote, you would be in the minority. Now think of yourself as a working cell of some other kind of entity, not even an entity, but something huge and dog-shaped. Recall if you will the Jeff Koons leafy dog that spent some weeks in Rockefeller Plaza maybe ten years ago. You saw it right? Go there now. Think of that dog being pulled through history on a leash and that is time. Imagine a model of dog, god, dog, god. Like that. Imagine its mind. You are in it.

On the cover of this book will be a picture that came to me one day and I[7] took it with my cell phone and it became my wallpaper. I looked at that picture daily until the end of Rosie's life and we shall say it is a photograph of an abstraction we are living in which is the universe and the dog's position in it. The dog stands between the darkness and light, the dog only knows. An earlier poet Rilke said this. What the Rilke did not know because there were not cell phones yet and so the union of the picture and sound was not yet complete (except in churches) is the fact that yes a dog was looking at death but in this photograph I share she is also looking beyond it at the light. And then the darkness again.

That is the procession of the universe, a system of stripes, or a time which is one of the codes of knowing. People like stripes. I urge you to read my talk on liking. Perhaps it is in here. Footnote maybe. It is essential. More than love. Yes. I suppose at the simplest level stripes are a picture of the sea. Also we may associate them with a nautical uniform. But because a navy's ultimate aim is destruction and death, to create higher and higher incidences of drowning we have to remember that the navy's use of stripes is not on the order of knowing but of seeing.

The navy, all navies are faulty reaches towards wisdom, the simplest reaches towards wisdom, the simplest fisherman or sailor is not, the scuba diver is not, though the touristy scuba diver is faulty, is hurting the coral that is related to foam which

---

7. Sometimes it is Rosie. She is [birthing] part of the popping motion that is foam.

I believe I may say quite a lot about in the past. I see foam as the subject of a book. Foam is pure knowing, foam is pure birthing, foam is a depiction of the supreme board without pictures. It is a dream of cells, a dream of being. And as you know the ocean is covered in foam and so is beer and that is very soon where I am going. The presentation on foam will be naturally incomplete. Necessarily. Even a wheel is full of holes. Spokes to turn . . . That is it.

My deep knowing about alcoholism and families and the genealogy of foam is limited to architecture sound and society mainly as it describes interiority and "family." I feel more comfortable than ever before when I talk about the coincidence of alcoholism in my family, for today I will discuss both my father's and my own because I am approaching the third ladder, or platform of life so henceforth (and turning back as you can readily feel) I name myself Bo Jean Harmonica.

The Order of Drinking (3-D)[8]

Some very large birds are nesting and flapping overhead, others are deep in the forest, tweeting. There is an army of good and it is birds. Dog and person of a mixed gender bow, handsomely. Hi. Thanks for hanging in. Forgive the chaos of my studio. It feels right to be speaking live with you from here. Takes a sip from a glass on the table next to her. A small dog bends down to his bowl. Lap-lap-lap. Water! Every day is a good day now. I used to drink and so did my father. Pulls a book off the shelf behind them. There are a lot of books about drinking. Puts it on the table beside her. Cheever's daughter wrote one and Cheever himself wrote only one. That's our core belief about his work. O'Hara too. John O'Hara. Certainty and singleness are such western pleasures and blessedly the drinker knows his purpose in life always. You could be sitting in a bar telling people that you are a juggler but in fact drinking is what you are doing.

---

8. Footnotes throughout courtesy of BJH. Personal testimony of "Eileen Myles" is lifted directly from her personal journals. I am Bo Jean and I speak anonymously.

Anyone can see this except another drinker and increasingly
the drinker spends their time only with drinkers so the seeming
is utter and increasingly the drinker just doesn't know. And if
you know a drinker you shouldn't bother to tell them. Throw
them in the gutter. Rich drinkers are the saddest of all cause
the seeing is utter; nobody throws them out and if they do any
work at all it is madness and only contributes to the density
of the culture. The culture's tendency to believe itself is particularly strong when it is wrong. And it gets shored up on the
inside. Have you yet had the dream about the simple thickness,
a dense and white humming substance like the catholic wafer.
That is the culture looming in, trying to r-r-rape you in your
sleep with its pictureless numbness. Watch out. What drinkers
call blackouts are really festivals of awful white density chewing
up everything in sight. The reason people have dreams about
losing their teeth is because on the dreaming plane teeth are
the only weapons against the thick coming fog, awe.

Awe surrounds angels, awesome is a good word to use to describe a thick pleasure—it's the holiness the thick-minded can
muster and there is the argument that any holiness is good,
but it's a fact that not everything is without scale: poetry, holiness, sex, nature. Less of these things or too much creates thick
states. Alcohol is one of them. Heroin. *It was awesome.* Fire
is one of them. Any fire is not a good thing. Weather is one
of these things. All these things need be entirely designed by
the participants or (in the cases of alcohol or drugs) I think
not practiced at all. It's a hard position yet I am very much
against the sameness of all things. That is thickness through
and through. Increasingly our world is run on this principle.

Why not? Those two words together make no sense. Don't ever use them in that way.

Eileen's father Ted, yeah that's what we called him, was an animal man. In his final months and days he growled around the house. A soaking wet glumness like all of Ireland governed his existence. Her mother, Genevieve, was partner to this Ted's dying and either should have had no partner at all ("Gen" aspired originally to be a nun) or one whose own stabbing need to be alive would have confused and startled her right out of her own tendency to always be ready for the dying. This dad had been such a man but he lost his wavy nature in the war. And then the alcoholic simply needs to stay wet until dog comes. The alcohol sloshes freely in the person's system until it is all there is and when it recedes the person begins to have visions they cannot stand.[9]

Therefore spiritual rehabilitative societies for the drinkers have come into being, *clubs*, and I, Bo Jean, have attended these. And I will share some intimacy about them as well I shall offer some new ideas for their improvement. The first one is this. Here I go. *Unh*. Get it. My *unh* changed the room. That's some of what needs to happen here. For the real time of this lecture you will be in the club. Forty minutes. Can you give me that.

The recession that creates the longing for Dog also should be covered in a procession of pictures. I will show you. [Pulls down.]

---

9. The father falling down in the Mar-Jon Motel in southern New Hampshire on a family vacation legs kicking and foam appearing at the corners of his mouth.

I understood [sip] the sea and the land when I was young because of charts that stayed open all day our eyes to drink in that
this is sea [slap] and this land [pound]. The phenomenology
of education is alarming. Children stand in the wee classroom
in their very first days with brushes and pots of paint, their
eloquent little fingers unloading the foam of existence onto
these flat portals that are developed in the schools. We call it
art. The information is later on posted taped up on the walls
of the classroom or the refrigerator of the child's home. And
that's it—end of story which represents a major loss. All the
information from these charts remains mute, unread, unless
the child is a lucky and future artist. The family saves it so
that it will turn up in some art books years later. This is true
in the case of Eisenman. Even here the information is read
wrong. Coy genius it is pronounced and not a guiding light of
the contemporary day. In the future I might even abolish the
category of art in order to put some things in their right place.

The next phase was dark. We deal now in specific experience.
Nonetheless useful. In old schools covered women with their
charts showed us saints, heaven and hell; devils, actual bald
devils with wings crawling up from a stinky underworld, under
your bed perhaps and these pictures too stayed open all day. Yet
there was very little connection between the two worlds. The
earlier one had us opening the pockets of our minds and now
they stuffed it with fear of Satan. Alongside those unrelated
maps of land and the sea. Satan is a thick creation. Geography
is a lie if not properly entwined with an understanding of Dog
and how *they* make the waters stop and start. We also need the
color. We need to encourage that nature of mind.

Yet later on these problems do begin to get solved.

Indeed the clubs the drinkers attend during the recession of their waters are highly evolved utilities where so much important happens—so much good. Love flows here and also writers develop novels & memoirs to sell to the world—but mainly these clubs create time.

You sit in your lovely prisons with your coffee on your metal chairs listening as one speaker after another faces "you" and tells you their story. You get up and get a cookie. You line the cookies on your thigh and you eat one after the other not paying attention to anyone except to hope they do not see your quiet chewing. You swipe the crumbs off your lap onto the floor. You spill your coffee, a milky puddle of coffee and crumbs surrounds your shoes and you sit there. Agog.

We call this agog listening. And you are learning here.

Because while someone at the table is speaking these cryptic charts flank them like in school. You have not seen the like since then and there's ten truisms on one side of the chart and ten on the other and one means the inside and the other means the out. There's an unrelated poetry to these.

The one about the outside is actually more interesting than the in, that's what we are learning but people feel that if they have to talk about the outside it has to be dull, as if the outside of these clubs ("the building") were a thick place and not insubstantially thin, absolutely nothing, totally and entirely transparent. Altogether the club is not boring. Indeed it's less adult than Disneyland and no fax of maturity either like so much of the culture. It's one of the most insubstantial and thin facilities on this plane(t) for instance you don't give it any money. It's like a machine you don't have to feed. This is the inconceivable thing. The club does not have to profit or multiply. This is spirituality. It's about recession an invisible thing, as pliable as the soul. It's the after, I don't think it's the before.[10] Mainly it is ultimately a place where you *know* you know less and as soon as you can picture anything at all it's where you go and the nature of this society is to operate exclusively this way yet I feel we could be informed so much quicker of all of this by pictures.

I think a nice big map of the world with "Dog" neatly printed on the water in an archaic font in one version [slap] and another on the land [pound] not much more complex than the ratty Christmas lights strung up and flickering in these rooms like a cheap bar so why not a glowing map deep and consciously plugged into how it actually is. Just a picture or a moving picture I don't care. I'm thinking dog stickers too. Stickers of Dog all over the map, in the bathroom, all over the world. Ones to take home. Put everywhere. Maybe ones just saying "bark."

People very often have a problem with the club because of "God." Nobody has a problem with Dog. You think this is a joke. Good. Laugh harder. Roll your eyes. Snort. This is not an airport. We need your love.

---

10. The before is a space in the club but it is w/out dog.

The text, the rolldown, we don't need at all. It's equivalent to the speaking. Love happens here. Drinkers find people to talk to and even have sex with and if the one you found is early in their recession the club says you are "elevening" them. You put your one against their one. The founder of the club himself was very much inclined to this. Look at the sad boozy eyes in the photos of him so often hung in the club and you think elevening and you think dog. I do. The belief is to be that kind of dog is wrong but everyone does it. I did it. You'll do it too. I'm proposing that we pull all the numbered charts right off the wall I already said and we let the love step be all. I don't mean go orgy with every shaky pigeon who walks in the door vision clouded with foam. 11 is dog that's all. 11:11 on your clock and you feel it. Right? And I mean love. Then we'll build a ship. That's the subtle meaning of what the "building" means. I'll take it slow.

I come from gratitude because the club is where I learned to speak, to do. It's where I first identified the capacity to *choose-listen*. Neanderthals had it. When we listen we are capable of using this ability (already installed) to intuit the diagram of the talk [*see fig. 1*] and also later [*see fig. 2*] the speaker is giving rather than to be trapped in agog time. Often children's paintings are of this thing. The over-seeing (or SFA—Seen From Above) came by way of dogs in space-ships aeons ago travelling above and transmitting maps which humans received as plaid and dogs intuitively know but even later with the invention of fire in the cave, what you got was just a grunty (but complex) diagram drawn by a stick in the dirt and not a lot of talk.

Maybe like this:

fig. 1

Or this.

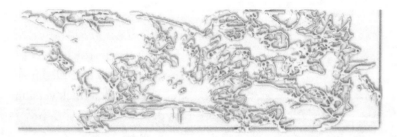

fig. 2

Feel it?

The mark about a thought was always a drawing not a word. When we say people need to be listened to we mean *felt*. They want their marks to get *in*. Go deep. The belief about listening inculcated in unwell families and school is that the person talking is an actual bag full of cogent & valuable information; the speaker is to be honored with obedient stares, even rhythmically averting your eyes to protect them from your intensity lest the speaker grow awkward and confused going um and ah; Yet we learn now, we try to waken & live for these moments. Lurch nod and bob when it happens. Grunt 'n groan. Receive. These are the nodes of communion, by which we get the plan, the living pattern in here and up above everywhere the speaker is spinning.

In the club we could easily project this pattern up on a screen. Imagine. It is both meditative and soothing. Without thinking at all to see how the speaker feels. Yet we already do know. We must dream, we must love. Tonight, today, the room where you sit is lousy perhaps the speaker having been taught by those who required the cheery *agog* listening in tandem with an aversion to yielding their own living pattern ("slick") thus a thick copy of knowledge has been transmitted to the speaker and extended now to us (yuck) by the speaker pounding on the table a thick version of the club's lore getting passed. No dog in sight. It's alright.

We can get to it, you can each one in all your own time can come our way. I myself developed choose-listening in my seat sitting there yes right next to you in the club. I say simply abide it. Eat cookies bob and flow. What I am developing please I have not developed alone. Choose-listening. I am only the first to name it.

We also call it seismic pattern. We call it junction or joinery.[11] Poets call it rhythm. My own belief is that all is nature, (and poetry) the nature of buildings, and trees of sex and of war. In all cases we observe the animal mind the person is jouncing without thought. Very often one is without. A person may be extremely thick and flat in terms of the content of their talk; a person can be out-and-out evil and maybe you've been wondering if there is such a thing. Yes there is. We all trade in it. We get on the subway. And we show it there. We shove and ignore. We kill.

If we didn't have a little experience of it how could it grow. How could it gain power. One of the great tragedies of our existence is that even dogs can be convinced to succumb to evil. Sorts of dogs are synonymized with evil, which is unfair.

---

11. The ecstasy "of" foam is that it is pure joinery.

Here I mean even the highest and the sweetest of dogs which Rosie was, one of the variety of dogs with the large elongated jaw, "the last fish" is what these dogs are called in the naming room of the supreme board. Operated by dogs and the pictures sent which as plaids are motes from that.

The board (and poets and dogs designated by the board) determines "true names" for aspects of existence that in daily rotation would simply become thick—they can't be used as *actual names* because they don't work. The way naming is determined is with a practical and transparent ordering of time in mind. A name reflects what is. If there is a deeper purpose to my telling here—and by "here" I mean inside the digits of this node, sagging, speeding iteration arising from a trove of science fiction, occasion of mold, fall perhaps into bathos; miracle. This is the tale of a dog written not solely, but perhaps skeuomorphically in order to articulate the enormity of just before and just after. The death of Rosie was a shrine of course, a bale of feeling, a stop-time but there's nothing actually to be learned from that. All of Rosie was a meeting place. As the now only always is. And I hope to find you now here too in this talk. I share my past, our hope.

In a spiritual situation I once asked a good man, a holy man named Paul[12] why I was absent in the significant moments of my life and he said what were the steps that brought you here. I sat agog. He looked at me. You were already gone.

---

12. Haller, in fact, and he is from this town where I write: Belfast, and that means get this "Mouth of the Sand Bar," a cabdriver told me this though he said "mouth of fish." Often the lie is better.

Today I feel the rapture of each of these mundane bricks. Each chapter, one moment, one building, one ship. Watch out! There are dogs on board. The road may be fouled. Where are you stepping now?

Time is an incessant building and knowing, hundreds of sandy steps. Jean is speaking for Eileen, I speak for Rosie, Rosie speaks for Eileen. Say Rosie is dying, say I, in my sand chair; she dies now, I mean you die, I die.

Iddy, Iddy, Iddy, Iddy.

I speak of our radiance, the agony of time and the mountain-ous and descending musik of the human scale. We need no torch. It's lit. Wuff I mean light; mean bed and I mean one little pumpkin face in a litter of puppies. Pretty little face. Rosie looked up on East 3rd Street one day and I heard call. I mean the joinery. And I heard it then. Each step its own tone, it's own truth.

There was a sign in Cambridge Mass. In the nineteen fifties. It was a billboard which I read repeatedly in the car on family trips when I was learning to sound words out. Even the Iron Curtain can't keep out ruth. My parents always laughed. The "T" had been crossed out. Who's Ruth I would ask. Why is there a billboard about her. [Smile.]

I am Bo Jean Harmonica. Who are you? What is your dog's name. I mean what is your dog name. Your true name. This is the call to power. Look at that beautiful grey sky full of storm.

See how poetry spatters, unmooring separateness—calling a boat "tree on water" overlaying one perceptual moment [Make pancakes with hands.] over another. "Tree" over "water" creates moving on it [hand roll] sailing, the human machine of being dog-like, paddling, two things at once then three.[13] This affords a breathing in time which can (I am getting there so long) produce a splendid node for a speaker of hate. Hate speech is wielded mainly by wounded lovers of power who defensively over-produce flatness[14] and thickness as an enormous anti-feeling blanket. The gratuitous result is that they are sometimes rendered as moving public speakers. And evil is just this accident perhaps. Awesomeness in the worst way. These speakers' seismic pattern is raggedly open and engulfing, sexual, persuasive, war-like and inestimably charming. They may put it to bad use. The woman-man! It is always true. Lesbians in the wrong body. Sometimes lesbians in lesbians. Clawing to get out. The female-female ones stay home become evil mothers. But more often these are men. Know that the same hidden unifying force is operating in all these people. Homeopathically in all people. *Know it.*

Cult leaders have it, all leaders do to some degree. I knew a man, Danny Krakauer, a poet and a postal clerk on E. 13th Street who heard Adolph Hitler speak when he was a boy. In Vienna. He said Hitler was riveting. His speech was largely composed of an erratic telegraphic popping. A misinformed flow amplified by irregular bursts of consonantal arcane verbiage

---

13. The fact that Jesus walked on water proved that he was god but also dog.

14. I want to propose a distinction between thickness and flatness together and the occurrence of flatness alone which is the innovation which inserts the three dimensional within the visual field. Even in my studio i.e. this "talk."

and the effect on crowds was to reduce their cells to that of a receptive and submissive child. Which is not so far fetched if we return to the scene (which probably seems like ages ago, perhaps it was) when the young George Bush in short pants climbed down off his presidential chair to get a big hug. Adolf Hitler's seismic pattern was apparently so strong that entire populations became that yearning and doleful boy. And Kurt Cobain (surely lesbian-lesbian) needed only to incant a few of his soft lamb lines ("I'm so horny . . . ") before his own very vulnerable fluid self his passive-aggressive nature miraculously transformed into an agonized and thrashing chorus of the underworld. This too I have confirmed from good witnessing. The Kim saw it. Kurt had the thickness. He was crouching behind the Courtney, a flat thick person as a non-feeling blanket to protect him from the foam of the communities he lost touch with as he cascaded ever higher and higher into the flatness of global success. (To die on the mountain!) He had to assassinate, he had to self-war. That was now. Time is moot. Here you stand waving your arms. Hello! I once saw Courtney on a stage after his death holding their baby child up to the audience like a camera. Do we have that film. We do. It is the meeting place and that is all. As Kurt said, *blam.*

The speaker is ignored. *You are sitting on your chair in the club.* I'm saying that pit bulls cannot be named "the last fish" because the rich complexity of the name begs time to think which publicly does not exist. We are making it now. Meanwhile the short thick word must be used: pit bull. It protects us from committing the crime of one who, with a little more knowledge, would only use it to throw something or somebody else overboard. A swift culture turns all things to the purposes of destruction or manipulation. I drag my foot. The tragedy remains: had Kurt been able to feel the thinness, the diaphany of time he might have been endowed with the eventuality of transformation. He felt power, and he roared because if not he'd be only lamb and something slimy and scary a bald devil on a chart perhaps would ravage and eat him. Tear him to bits. Choose-listening might have been Kurt's salvation. It wouldn't have saved my father, they both were lambs, yet Kurt was a true shepherd, my father was not.[15] Hitler was no shepherd. No lamb. And we know from all of their notebooks that all of these men were immersed in a sea of pictures, the speaking and singing and roaring came right out of their drawings.

15. He drew Kilroy in my drawing pad.

Hitler's drawings from the earliest were already ill-focused, bad seeing. In World War I dogs did important work in the field of battle, and Hitler was also such a messenger. He did a dog's work. If they didn't have a dog they would use him. That's history. How much would have changed if one dog one day did not show up. I push Rosie's ass into its gap in time. Like Shelley Winter's giant butt in *Poseidon Adventure* (the wildness of the drive-in). I speak of fat for a reason. In choose-listening we learn to randomly palp the fat of the story, *tap, tap,* zooming in on the heft of the speaker's content, yet largely ignoring it, thereby gaining access to the pool of seismic attention, time as a warning or warming.

We follow the speaker and their shifting states, look at their shirt (do I want it?) carefully examining their shoes, taking their pulse in terms of the rhythmic pitch, the seismic by which we know what is going on in the ocean on earth right here in the room in terms of information mattering. Each of us is a cell of that potential knowledge cluster, that mammoth green dog being lead right now through the cosmos.

More and more of us came and the patterns got swifter and the knowing entirely disassembled and we will never reassemble it again but instead we now return to knowing's just before. It is attractive.

To add. I did this in my childhood too. And you too else you would not be here. In adulthood we must relearn the wisdom of the young who feels her inside while she is being taught she is wrong. To abide in the totalitarian, to survive one must look straight into the face of the nun or whoever and muse. Yet this brought so much upon me. Warily I learned to not absorb their enmity. Choose listen.

I am like you. Innocent. I am confused. I am greedy. I am impatient. I sat in the club with my cookie and felt bored. My waters recede so slow. And colors brightening around me. I feel my body. I'm a man but there's a woman in it. Drugs don't drive my menses. A crazy new thought. The mood does.

I bleed.

I flow.

Grumpily I want to speak. I watch them perform. I did not know I was Bo Jean yet. Like you I arrived in my seat through a miracle.[16]

I wandered in through the tall metal gates on an autumnal evening was it 1982 or '83 into the strange topiary of a West Village church yard the very landscape evoking a petite Versailles thereby filling me with a great sorrow for all the poor of Europe and that producing a beeping moving spot (observed by dogs overhead) quickly installed on the map of secret royalty: son/daughter of my father who like the inbred heirs of the continent and Ireland could not chew. Kurt Cobain, I should mention, died with a full fine set of teeth. Yet Courtney Love did all the biting. That is a failed system. So many other parallels flood into my mind right now. I stay simple. I won't detail the fascinating overlays of rape and inferior seeing and puppet sex that favored the emergence of the disintegrated jaws of the Bourbon royalty, a cherished example. Though consider. When you say someone has a weak jaw, you are also implying that they (and their line) are on its way to extinction. On all planes. Men grow beards popularly now to hide their dying.

Buoyantly we recall that the pit bull has a strong and superior jaw. My father came back as such a dog whereas at the time of his death he had no teeth. I recall the gleaming dentures he often presented to me as warning (superior teaching) and

_____

16. Eileen's story. No. BJH is anonymous.

because of which I never went to the analyst, the psychiatrist, shaman or the priest but always and only the dentist instead.

I said Abba. I was an errant cell squirreling into the club.

People had been losing their teeth for hundreds of years in Ireland, that was the plan, because a toothless nation has no purchase on awe, the thickness will quickly come and surround everyone hence the phrase: "a thick mick." Part of the curse of the Tuatha Dé Danann![17] Tooth loss is surely a corollary of the eventual unknowing, the drunkenness, the whole frothing lot of it.[18]

Sitting in my metal chair "I" felt gripped by sorrow. If only I could speak. I called upon the power of the fairies to let me feed these herds—mentally ill and the leaden, the stylish agog triumphant (a final stage—to be avoided at all costs) to be catalytic; help me produce the grey, charm the room. I listened so careful to what each said the ritual being one would speak for half an hour and the rest of us were frozen in place with our cookies, coffee (the room billowing with smoke) while a

---

17. Fairy culture.

18. The same forecast of toothlessness is true for the American Indian. To be prisoner on your own land is to be raped of your pride. The thickness will soon descend. The American Black exists on an entirely different platform of pain. To be taken from his or her home, from your home, then be prisoner elsewhere is to be slave, then pet. The result is unholy, both for the captives and the host country (US) also often wholly erased like the rape victim. There is too much to be said on this subject here but it can be summed up by the fact that this kind of robbery is cellular. It assaults everyone's pride, eventually. Except for dogs to whom we pray.

man babbled on. A woman spoke about being depressed for fifteen years after which she went into a mental hospital. I was horrified. And enthralled. How can *I* get in on all the divulging. It's my thing. Surely I will be lauded and since I am true poet my language nature will inevitably vibrate on a higher subtler plane. For nights and months I was ringing, churning, screeching and up-rooted; re-routed continually by the aleatory raising of hands. I drew a breath. I felt sure it was time to jump in. The club was my teacher. My moment had come. I had been silent now for about seven years.

Rosie was a puppy in 1990 and I broke the rules once in a while and took her with me to the club and she wandered about the room being adorable, collecting pats and hugs. I was as usual deep in my process of sculpting a moving response to the speaker, up in my head like a depressed light house keeper in cool sneakers angling to ever so carefully slip my own sentiments up over the speaker's story like an invisible mask through which my wisdom could slyly enter (a giant face) and take over the room. In my mind I was already talking, had been for years, and I imagined people being patient with me tonight if I spoke and that felt good and in that moment the speaker kindly looked at me. Simultaneously a thought struck. Cause I hadn't seen Rosie for a while. Oh no.

What if she pooped.

Then the guy at the front of the room said you, fascinated I think by my sudden look. What do <u>you</u> have to say. The meeting was almost over. The pitch of the moment was so complete I could only divulge what was true.

Well that's my puppy Rosie walking around and . . . I was just wondering if she already had shit on the floor. The room roared. I had shared my vision with them for the first time, the uncollected thought and my wanting and my trying and my desiring was over at last and now finally I was in.

In where. Well anywhere. I was in the room sure but I was also gone, totally lost. Speech arises and passes swiftly in the vapors of transition. I don't know who spoke that night. I never would know her again. She was nobody I was in control of. How could it be true, this complete surrender of one's own mind and the reality of opening it momentarily to everyone and how was this even desirable.

You know the expression Elvis has left the building. It includes its opposite. When he entered he changed the room. He left and he changed it again. The thought that breaks both ways is equally holy. And it's a holy space. That's why the club is good. It's not a prepared thing, the coming and going. It is the unexpected guest. Always all of us there were listening. And if you sat tight holding on to every single precious word of the person in front of you there's no room for that sudden visitation. A thought is an angel. A prophet. When I say "I am

one" I mean I am like everyone. Or anyone you didn't invite.
Who was suddenly present.

In choose listening we empty our minds of presence and
absence, of poetry as it relates to actual speech, as place as
opposed to time. Which is today. No it's not. It's the junc-
ture. Today is a postcard slid in from just before and some
saw it coming, and some of them are here and some of the
people have not yet come. How can we possibly unite all
those groups. We can't. We can only open ourselves to the
true and actual pictures in our own consciousness and through
our participation in this endless corridor we discover at last
that we are not alone. Is a dog turd lying on the floor. In the
moment of the room's laughter absolutely yes it was. We all
constructed that poop together unexpectedly. That is the true
ship. That is the only kind of knowing I am talking about.
Goodbye. See you later!

Once you get this you are dog. Some get it occasionally. It
is their one story. Others got it once and their friends who
never got it like to tell it over and over again. The word
enthusiasm refers to the early Christians who first got dog
and they just couldn't stop talking about it. History will say
it was Jesus Christ but I'm saying the only kind of thickness that can truly transport a group of persons from here
to there is the word "dog" which provokes laughter unlike
god which produces awe, anger (which god) or contempt
for all religion is secularism. Which is capitalism whether
they name it god or not. We think of capitalists as digging
a hole. Why bother when you can get a dog to dig that hole

for you. Think of the prophet Rosie smiling. I dig you she says. Put that on a button. This is that club which I am imagining. Join us now.

Everybody wanted to know what kind of dog the president in 2008 would get and this is presented in the media as (tee-hee) the um humorous end of the news item (yeah how about the end of the world, you idiots! . . .[19]) yet we refer to that dog as the bishop and that dog is carefully chosen. Oh you can't imagine for how many thousands of years.

It is a political dog. Certainly if the right dog had been in the White House during the Bush presidency the whole Serpent Queen moment might not have even begun. Jimmy Carter wouldn't have had sex with a snake. There was no precedent for it.

Eileen Myles you might remember made a fool's run up to the presidency (1991–92) with Rosie in mind for the bishoprix but it did not succeed. Sadly it was a little too obvious.

It's a long moment the cross insemination of galaxies and it can still be stopped. In the simplest way. It can be slowed. How long is now. Think about it. Rosie is no longer with us as an entity but more like a holy card, a living picture on a chart. If I can explain the nature of a political animal, which she was, and situate her correctly in the current constellation of galaxies,

---

19. How about the constant end which is war. War for resources, usually defunct juices and gases singing deep under the surface of the earth and the dogless capitalists squeeze it again and again like an orange until there is none. Only a husk of a planet where we live—without dog.)

here in New York, in America, and in North America, the
Western Hemisphere, in Ireland and Istanbul and Florence,
in Belfast and Morocco, even MacDowell colony of Southern
New Hampshire[20], and Marfa TX, sweeping the Earth and
going across. . . galaxy number one, galaxy number 2 . . . so
on to 18, animating all and

      coming back then cause you know
          cause you know
            cause you know
    cause you know
       cause you know
              cause you always have to return.

---

20. A healing place.

XXXX

A man with grey hair walks down a dirt road. He utters uh. Sometimes a moan or a muffled sound and he lights a cigarette. His gait is slow, he doesn't stumble but there's almost a stutter in his walk. Next to him is a woman with her grey hair tied up in a messy bun. She wears a black teeshirt and is largely silent and the man points things out to her from time to time. The light is extremely bright. It's hot. They're examining an excavation. He points to a sculptural plaque with bodies, gods probably. She grunts appreciatively. They walk around. The houses are yellow, and there's bright orange flowers like morning glories lining the fences of the neighborhood—neither rich nor poor though probably both. The yards are all dedicated to a craft manufacture (tiles) so there are hunks of quartz sitting on pedestals. It's a holiday. No one's around. The man stops and lights a cigarette. He groans. The woman asks him something and he seems indignant. He reddens. She grows quiet. The sky is a deep clear blue. The trees are at the height of their prowess. It's summer and they sway in the slight wind of the day, about noon. The two seem barely related but together for purposes of their own. He sometimes

eyes her after a bit of witticism and she stoically observes him
without scorn not giving a proper foil either. She thinks this
is her dignity. He thinks she is boring. That's how it looks.
It's like we stepped out of the movies and landed in another
one. Exactly that. This one feels reddish, maroon and faded
somehow even in its brightness. The people walking one another are later in life, she clearly in better health than him. She
says something about the orange flowers. He shakes his hand
to deny it, dismissing her thought. She relapses into silence.
They stand in front of a larger bush with pink flowers. He
presents a theory. She says something else. He shakes his head
in disagreement. Both of them admire a blue wall. Him first
though she had been thinking about it. Now her appreciation
sounds false. She takes a picture. He hates her. Lights another
cigarette. At a certain point as he's pointing out the marbled
sub-structure of the falling down walls she asks him to repeat
something. He does—with mild condescension. She is unable
to hear the words he says. She asks him to repeat the words.
He mocks her strongly saying the words in a tone that suggests
that the listener is an inattentive fool. Later she will insist he
treat her with some respect but now she is stunned that he feels
so entitled to enmity he even will direct it at her. The pattern
continues in different settings for about three or four days.
The man attempts to buy cigarettes in a small wooden hut.
The young man in the green teeshirt seems unfamiliar with
the words. The man repeats himself. The young man shakes
his head. The older man does the same exaggerated performance of the name of the item he desires and the young man
pulls it out of his shelf looking slightly intimidated, no just
paler somehow less present but his dark eyes quickly sail to

the woman's and he smiles and she liquefies her eyes to say she agrees. It's unclear if the older man observes this performance. At night they walk along a promenade filled with families and teenagers. At one point she asks him about his family and he tells her a sorrowful story about his father and then his sister too. He relates these events to times in his life, in both their lives when they met. They both think in some way about how you never know about the tragedies in the lives of the people you live around. They actually don't know each other at all having met thirty years earlier in the city. He might have liked her then if she had been willing to let him amuse her. She disliked how easy things came to him when he was newly arrived from another town and she wonders if she will have an opportunity to tell him this. When she looks back on the trip she still sees the trademark tiles of the town on the public wastebaskets and continue to wish she could have one, could buy it or steal it. Why don't they sell them she wonders but the charm is that the basket is just sitting there and they value this too. It would be like going into someone's house and wanting to buy their wastebasket. She thinks of their long slow walks in the late morning midday sun around the old monuments and the yellow houses one of which he purportedly came here to buy. He's going to die she thinks. When they pay their bill at the hotel restaurant his liquor bill is enormous though he didn't seems to be drinking all day long. He had another way it shows right there on the bill. When she drops him in the cab they talk quickly and angrily to each other because he doesn't know exactly where she is going though he had given the driver the address. She can't understand why he is upset. He is going home to the bad smelling apartment where he will die.

Peel

Turn off the sound. And the peacock feather falls onto the keyboard. *Its eye blue staring at me in a block of sun.* I shove it away.

Each love, each yard yellow flowers each fence each hose. Each blue bucket each mailbox each potted plant. Stalling. The leaning white board with orange emergency stripes. We look to accommodate the pace of her body. These rungs the only way we go. To magnify her. Behind the fence and mulch pattern of berries something red. I feel like a cop. Looking for the rhyme in flowers berries thrown down in the yard. I can't write. I always want to feel your large head and go dog. A truck backs up. This empty street covered with spots. *Flutters.*

Here is the dog. Tiny paws on the side of the screen her shadow leads at a decent pace. Suddenly even wheels hubcaps are interesting. A ring a shallow cup around a central gleaming circle. The hub! And a leaf falls in the still life of the world. And you muscle around a yellow fireplug. And the tree sticks its legs in the air. Horny for meaning. For day. Oh fuck and the phone wires so slouched. That's lyric. While you stall the world's a bit capsizing.

We cross the street. It's like water ballet this intersection and the silent cars all white.

If I add something it changes and I'll work with the new accord. If you would come back after these white flowers. I want you again. We tunnel right into them and their yellow heart. It's the slowest thing.

Whirling around. Closing in and you're a bundle of leaves and flowers over a wall your shadow too everything looks like old slip covers. *Give me my dog.* Start there. And for one careening moment she's here.

Transcribed in Istanbul, August 2013

Dog House

Ireland, 2013

"Rachel?"

"Marie?"

"Laura?"

"Rose?"

She was peeping out the window.

Knock Knock Knock.

One of the two men outside waved from beyond the gate.

She's not going to come out said one of the men.

Well what's she doing said the other.

She's got babies said the first one.

Doesn't mean she can't open the gate.

This is definitely the house.

Is that *a house*.

The first one put his sneaker on a part of the fence and lifted himself up. He began taking pictures with his phone. Holding himself up with one hand and trying to take the pictures with a finger of the other. The pictures were bad.

This is definitely the house.

You think it's a house.

She's coming.

He kept taking his pictures then he jumped down.

Hello the girl called.

May I help you she said.

The inside of the house was open to the yard. Plastic chairs tipped, a long shelf on the wall and a mirror over it. A sickly blue green wall. Was the fuzzy pink stripe a piece of his arm. That's cool. He sort of liked the bad pictures better. The stripes of the fence weaving unceremonious like an amusement park ride. The picture making him think strangely of what he saw on twitter the day before. A girl's mouth with someone's dick in it and her eyes looking up at all the world and the man's flat stomach viewed like the fence. I guess *he* took the picture.

May I help.

The long haired guy tried to explain—

—<u>Hey</u> said the grey-haired one.

Long haired one mimes "I stand corrected."

My family used to live there.

This is not my family the young woman said. She had black hair, long, and she was a little plump. No she was young.

I'm sorry I saw you up there with your babies.

There aren't any *babies* up there.

I don't have any babies.

I'm sorry I thought maybe you were baby-sitting—

I'm 20. I wouldn't have any babies.

"Elaine."

The house torn open like god's ass. And the roof torn off a lot.

Yeah that's the roof.

Now they were sitting in the car. That's how most of these houses used to be built. Grass bursted out of the old stone sides of the house. Then he was circling. Click click click. He had to get *something*.

Are you sure this is the one. I don't think—

You should ask Jackie. She lives right up there around the bend. House with the electric fence.

He was trying to picture.

Can you open the gate so I can go in.

I can't.

That dog is the problem.

Bark. Bark. Bark.

Oh yeah. His name is Casey. He is the noisy one.

Yeah he's been barking since we got here.

Who do you think—

I think my grandmother lived here.

She looks at him like he's crazy. No she's a little interested.

Thank you for letting us bother you—

Sorry, we're —

Hah. I'm doing nothing. I saw you getting up on the fence.

Well I was trying to see. So I can't get in—

This dog is the problem.

He can't be with the others.

How many dogs do you have in there.

Hunters bring them.

Oh I don't know she laughs. I think there's three.

No seven.

My father lets them stay.

This is where they leave their dogs when they go hunting—

It's <u>hunting</u> <u>season</u>.

She doesn't know what that is. She shrugs.

The long haired one smiles.

It's <u>always</u>. There's no *season*. There's just one season he chuckles.

Really?

So you're related—

My grandmother was a Riordan.

Or an O'Riordan.

I'm not family she said.

Of course she could have babies. He liked that she laughed at that—

She must have *something* in mind.

No just you know hanging around the house.

Just dogs here.

That's all the house is now.

My father's going to fix it up.

Go talk to Jackie.

The electric fence—?

There's just a lot of crap out in the yard. God's asshole. White stuff and old wood. There's a square where the bed used to be. Wall's falling down. That's all there is.

At the lake the woman was walking back with a large group of them in brightly coloured parkas. They like colours. Someone suggested they stop for a photograph. They stopped near the pond. The artist did. Because she had an idea. Later on she gave him a drawing. Was that the last time I was her. A little two inch figure. That I have a portrait of her. An innocent doll. They were going to hear some music.

Can we talk, she said.

I don't have so much time. I can call you back.

No for a second. There's something I need to talk to you about. I don't know how this happened.

He died in the house. Benny did. Peter found him. He had been there for days. That was the beginning of Peter's drinking. And of course Benny had the bleeding ulcers.

We have that too. My brother had it.

She shrugged.

He's got a few cows now.

Peter does.

It was very hard.

He was young.

He used to ride a motorbike.

He liked that very much.

We wouldn't see him for a while and then he'd turn up.

We figured he was drinking.

He didn't say much. He was quiet.

I'll have to check the date.

I don't know how this happened. I was in his apartment. We were kissing and touching each other. I started it—

I have to go hear some music.

I can't believe you're going to go hear music now.

I think it's a really good thing.

It's beautiful like God's asshole torn right open. To the day. And now dogs live there. That one bastard—

Peter was bad for a few years after that. Barney was the father's name.

Why do I feel my family is here.

Birmingham. Annie was there. I see Rosie in her eyes too. I see my father.

Turns her head like that she looks like Aunt Annie—

and you think they'd be John Joe's—

don't you. There were no.

Can I talk to him.

Timothy, Timothy was my father.

I think before him. Like there was an older sister who went to America. Ellen. Nellie.

No. there weren't any others. I don't think so.

It was *famine*. Everyone was gone.

He delivered mail.

The one little house. Certain dignified sides. Almost a drawing of a house, a hole in the stone, and cementing, and some lightening on the right. The day pale blue, hardly blue and the scratchy red corrugated roof. Like it has sky too painted on, but it's just metal, whatever it is, broken faded.

She came back out. *What was her name?*

Thought you might want this. That's its name. That's the old name of the house:

"Gleann Alainn"

Knocknagoun,

Rylane,

Co Cork

You can find it on Google earth just the house, this house isn't there. It's there all alone.

It means beautiful view.

Jonathan: you should describe the scene from outside. First what it would look like to a person watching.

From the outside.

Yes he said. From the outside.

And then something not human.

But alive you mean.

Yes something alive but not human.

And then a thing.

A tree?

A bucket?

Three perspectives.

I took the old dog, the bad dog from so far away. He would *see* a man trying to get into his yard, hopping up, making himself tall clicking with his hands and later he would feel that person walking by a lake and the clicking thing makes a chirping sound the man holding the thing making no sounds to his head fast and choppy and not heavy but then he is asked to hold something. A bucket? A big proud sad thing.

Now. He is holding it now. The dog feels a fence in the man. The man's climbing down and he is now in a small area. He is watching someone carrying something dangerous with their eyes closed shut. They are trying to make the man watch them hold it and they are suddenly very happy to hold it it is a glowing thing and the man wants to turn away and he opens the gate and closes it.

This is what tragic means. That's what he tells her. That there's doors that really close.

She wondered what Peter saw. Would he tell her. He was a boy. Well he was in his late twenties. Everybody in the little town would take the man's son into their houses and make him some tea. Often he had no shoes. We all did then. We knew he was your son. Yes he came here once in a while. It wasn't *for* him. They looked around the room.

The dog just wanted all of us to go away. It was *his* yard.

You know Casey right Rose.

I do.

The tree has been here for so long so if it feels a woman coming up from the lake, it feels the lake and it can feel a group of
people, but maybe not one person, it can feel the phones in the
place where the phone nearby is receiving it and it can feel the
resistance to the distance rays and the pressure arising to stop
it, to ask it, the pressure breaking down, the quickening when
the far away sounds hold on shaking something a convoluted
energy wanting to relieve itself and rocking back and forth for
a while in the cold when each leaf and all the leaves fall. If the
tree over there suddenly didn't know how its leaves started leaving it but where could it have been in all the risings and fallings
that happen inside where had it been why did it want to be
seen now lightning becoming naked and an alone tree is there
such a thing now here except in the old sad gem of the telling.

A cigarette parks in and out of lips watching the intense rag-
gedy woman receive the call from far away and the cigarette
smoke is pulling down into a chest as the eyes of the woman
look around getting slower. The lips about to receive the warm
paper as the woman seems to drop into her own body cavity
to let the facial expression a little tighter almost happy to be
told that the thing she saw approaching now blazingly here the
lips almost kiss the cigarette as the woman says you love him
and the energy on the other side echoes. The smoke blowing
against the pinkening sky as the woman looks at the door into
the building and feels the music and describes the door to the
cell phone and the cell phone can't understand why there is a
door there now but there is. And she is going through it, slow.

Far away a woman falls backwards on her bed in much brighter light and pats her dog.

Bernadette. I think it might have been Bernadette.

No it was Rebecca. And she was laughing now and holding her hand to her hair and her mother Veronica was there and there were seven dogs all of them theirs. Red dogs and white dogs. One dog sits in a truck. The bad one. And the small boy, Darragh, led us into the shed. It was different people now. The men were gone. The bed was there he said pointing with a stick. That's original. The white and green dresser sitting against the wall. He watches her mouth open. That's not true. It would be more like and she pointed at something old and brown. More like that. She's with Deirdre Powers. And the twilight setting in. And both sides of the street were theirs. It was referred to as the shed. It was out of great respect and John Joe's home would not be torn down but it was the shed and the dogs lived there. Eileen Lynch says do you know who this is. Yes I have definitely seen this before and I don't know who she is but I do *know* this. You don't know who this is. It's Helen. Because Eileen Helen Ellen it's all the same. It's one name. She smiled. Are you married. I said no. She smiled. She glimmered and crinkled. And her brother did too. It runs in the family she smiled. And it did.

I am one of them now. He was tall, very tall and powerful and he loved the Gaelic language and poetry and he could recite it for hours. He had a beard. And at that age (91) you could count the white hairs in his black beard and his head. His name was John. Jack O'Riordan. Are there pictures. No there are no pictures. And she smiled. These are the pictures. That would be her little boy. Do you know which little boy this is. I do not know. He would be her little boy. I can't keep this. You have it. These are your parents. Right. Yes they are. Then they sat on the mantle like they were always standing there. Benny's mouth is open.

And Peter is preparing the landing strip. He saw Benny. The location is no longer receiving information. Possibly they feared he would just write about them like he did with his whores and the young drunken woman shaking her tits they just didn't want to be lied about. After all they were family. And what about the old woman in the hospital. Nellie. It was too hard to see. He read that the paternal grandmother will tell you how you are going to look. He laughed when he pictured himself in a scarf like his farther. The women so often protected them. The land was bad. It was a manner of slavery. They might pay you in drink to work. Not even an animal. More like an angel who exchanges work for going away. Getting lost in exchange for it. All of them.

He was found in the other house and his mouth was open. It was an O surrounded by an O and one was brown and one was green and it got wider and wider eating up the entire house and the field. It was the kind of O that would tear up your face and your hair fell in and all your clothes. The bed he was lying on was gone. It was an entire hole. And the stove. Everything wavering and greenish. That's how it looked. And the land and the trees. He wavered back into the house and the mouth like a clown's mouth, he looked like a black man and the earth. He wasn't human. And all of him was huge and bursting out of his clothes like rags. He had stopped for a couple of beers. He had a kit bag. He went back and got it and crouched on the floor. The room stunk. It stunk to high hell. He didn't have eyes. His eyes were torn open. His hair—he sipped his beer. He would begin planning the field. I thought I might get a few cows he told the hole. The hole stared. I thought. I wanted to talk to Peter about what he had seen because he had my whole life. Did I just want to see death. Why would I just want to go in the ground. Did you see it Peter. And what was it like for them. Did he blow the house down with his explosion. I had it too and I wanted to see what it was like for him. Up there in their ships they can see what we do. Peter moves the cows around. We are organizing the yards and the fields so that the ships can come. His mouth is open like a hole like a signal. He is huge and he is breaking the house. Peter staggered out. He stood in the field. He counted his cows. He looked up. He was waiting for them.

"The Dog's Journey"

I've been gone from your life for seven years. But believe me—I am keeping an eye on things. I notice a chapter on your list called "The Dog's Journey." I read it and think: I can help. I know I'm the dog being referred to *and* I'm a pit bull. We love to work so I will help you get the thing up and running and on its way around the world. *Afterglow* is totally a book with legs (four if I can be dumb) so it will go a lot further than your earlier Eileen-based fictions. "The Dog's Journey" is, as I envision it, is a big chapter, maybe the last. You've got that look of fear on your face, Eileen. Okay I know you don't like to get pushed around. I'm not doing *that*. But I most definitely am dogging you. You need it. Here's the plan.

Imagine this chapter as a tapestry. Seriously, because a dog going on a journey sounds like a kid's book. Cartoon, most likely, and a couple of celebrities will be doing both of our voices and you won't have any control over that so my advice Eileen is for you to step back a little . . . go to the 19th century *which you love* or even the 14th which was really the day the hey day of tapestry. Tapestry is absolutely the way to go for this chapter. It's a literature I'd like to rub up against. Any dog would. Tapestry is toney it will absorb what we give it. I'd like to pee on this chapter frankly. I would like to tear it to shreds. A tapestry is bumpy and nubby even stinky like a couch and a dog loves a couch. I'm thinking of course of the purple one you have had in storage for eight years. It could have been in the chapter where you listed my stuff. Because it was *my* couch. I simply loved it, it was *us*.

The couch was the place where you finally fought back. It was so cool and so modern even you couldn't accept I had torn it to shreds. It was your *California* couch. So after my attack you had it covered in lavender marine quality fabric so I could no longer open it. We hit rock.

But back to our tapestry. Or *r-r-r-rugs*. I know you were mulling the idea of a wraparound. Not a <u>skirt</u> but something cozy you know like a narrator at the top of each chapter so it'd be palatable for the sophisticated reader. They'd feel comfortable since it wasn't for them. People are always happier with someone else's shit—kitsch is that way. They feel smart peeping over somebody else's shoulder—kids always. So *nice* they have this good show. So a smart dog book for kids makes a lot more sense than a stupid dog book for adults. But you know <u>Jethro</u> (if I may?) your work already has a YA quality because of how you like it to be readable which is a bit like chewable . . . and that's good. But a kid tone won't work, then. See, cause you're <u>already</u> there.

I have one more thought which is dog ghostwriting. Think of it. Funny to ghostwrite for a dog. And a course then you

can be all snarky about rock stars with ghostwriters. Not Kim
but you know the other ones. You liked being my ghostwriter.
And you were always that. But, as you pointed out to that Irish
writer, Dave, when he brilliantly proposed he write a chick lit
book—uh Dave *all* men's books are chick lit. Every woman
in literature is some guy's notion of how women think. Men
invented the genre (calling it literature) yet when women write
books they get cordoned off as *chick lit*. Where is dick lit I ask?
I'm female too Jethro. I get all this.

"Dog ghostwriting"—great language, funny idea, but honestly
aren't all dog books dog ghostwriting. No dog writes a book,
no dog wants a book written no dog reads a book and the only
part that might be interesting is the idea that all writers are
ghosts. Look at you! The writer spends her life reducing her
own existence to that of a ghost. All the vitality floods onto
the page while her own existence grows wanner and thinner.
Writers are pale, spooks so to speak. Your time is winnowing
to a close and you've spent a great chunk of it sequestered in
rooms creating your double. To this dog, Rosie Myles, your life
was a dream. *Mine wasn't!!* So let's finish this baby and wake up.

I mean the point is to dissolve categories. Ideas hold things
up. Eileen—just write. It's that simple. I will. Look at that
tree moving out there. All that bobbing, all that bird song. It's
paradise. Work with me.

A tapestry is a great way to describe my journey inside and out
because it's easy. You must first make a cartoon then the weaver
fills it in. That's you. You're the weaver. I'm the cartoonist.

Moi and Raphael. Nice company. I think this tapestry is what you've had in mind for a very long time. It's a deep emotive process. And fortunately you've even got weavers in the family, in Ireland, which is to say you come from a line of receptive people, thank God.

In Arlington when your father came falling off the roof . . . when he hung so stilly in the air *as if* he was held aloft by threads . . . well he was. Dog tapestry! When life sends pictures you can't digest quickly enough you convert them to a cartoon mechanism so that the colors become very hard and strong. Very clear so you can abide them. Think of the work of Rainer Werner Fassbinder. Heavy shit. Same deal. Always each image leans on the other held abreast by wefts and warps so the shock of reality really gets caught. Held. On this tapestry your dad (who is kind of me) is still hanging in the air over your head. That tarot card feeling you had about his death was true! And here's me, my dog self, down there low and central & bursting out of my mother's insides. A little splatter actually looks good on a tapestry. Feel the texture. Right at the bottom of the carpet. And there I am dying in the vet's office on University *in* the very sleeping bag which you carried me in. I kind of knew something was about to happen but I kept chewing. I felt weak. Food is like a good book. That body was done.

Everybody's life is just this kind of picture. People get dogs to help them construct it. Feel it Eileen. Heart to heart. The energy bounces—becomes apparent. So this is the template of our relationship, exposed, right here. Like a poem and waaay better than a movie or a kid's book. Because this story, the dog's journey, I cannot say often enough, is true.

I notice that you've been sleeping in it, in that sleeping bag for inspiration. That's good. We can reproduce that slimy royal blue fabric. And, here. The brown. I'm eating some very tasty carne asada out of Anna Joy's hand; not yet dead. The weft is like this. Discontinuous. And here's Ali's big beautiful face looming over the spectacle of my dying. Ali looks good on a tapestry doesn't she. Some people were born for this medium. She would look good on a mosaic too. Has any dog's death been honored this way before. I feel like a funeral director. Lot of funeral directors are dogs. The Grannan family in Arlington. Remember them. I think they were mainly terriers. Anyhow. I knew their son. I don't want to get distracted. We'll stop and we'll start. We've got a lot of territory to cover but I promise you we will nail it by the end. Will Hank end the show? (Exhales.) I just don't know. Stuff changes . . .

Right now I'm thinking he should come earlier. I think he will slow things down if we put him in right here. Yip yip yip. I saw that little bubby in action.

The pit bull walks over to the carpet on the wall. She gets up on her hind legs and she pushes up the edge of the tapestry a little bit. The underside shows.

It's a maze of pulled threads, colours. *This is what I mean.* In terms of story, the front of the carpet, we're taking moments and we're freezing them. An entire existence. Right to the tiniest stitch. Yet the whole thing is mobile. She gives the thing a shove and it shakes and buckles. *Look.* Everything does.

Eileen: Wow.

[Nods, knowingly] Good I'm glad you're speaking up. I don't want you feel silenced by this chapter and I certainly don't want you sliding stuff in later on because you felt silenced. [Shrug.] It's totally what the little monks did when they were copying the bible. More history! The 14th century when the tapestry (aka *rug*) came into prominence was a time full of trauma. The plague (in Europe) and no one could read and the church kept sending out all these dire images of heaven and hell. Inside of the church. For the rich it was mainly in private spaces. Lot of these tapestries were from the New Testament and "The Hunt" was also a big one. Most famously "The Hunt of the Unicorn." Which was totally about policing gender. They used a young virgin with braided hair to trap the pansexual unicorn. I can't even stand to look at those tapestries. It hurts.

The king had many houses. And look out the window—yeah where you are is fine. There's always a lot of houses. Up the hills. Lot of apartments. A lot of worlds. *Capisch?* Any tapestry is made to be peeled off the wall like a dream and carried someplace else and opened up there. Henry VIII had like two hundred and fifty tapestries which to me seems vulgar. He didn't have that many hearts. He didn't have that many minds. But that's a king. It *looks* like he did. And the tapestry finally does contain the soul of the weaver *and* the cartoonist *and* the king. That's the miracle.

OK back to my birth. This little dog face peeping out. Right there. That's me getting born. But Lucy's cunt was not a movie theater. It was more of a *fundus*. You know. It's like uh . . . a *stomach* and you're in the back and then you gotta imagine there's like an opening on the opposite side. That's us. Right here where we're standing. We're *in the world*. This is a *picture*. A deep illusionistic one.

OK so here's a little later on . . . I'm in a litter on a city sidewalk. East 3rd Street. We'll put an actual street sign in. Make it real. I'll just stick a toothpick in for now. I'm with my brothers, my one little sister and I'm literally *woven* to Lucy. That's my mom. A beautiful dog. A big white dog right [pounds] in the middle of the carpet. Those soft faded black spots. Just a few. Excuse me. I'm tearing up. I was born on a sidewalk. Maybe I was born on the roof. I don't know. I'm fatherless of course. It's what all of you increasingly have in common with us. Think about it. Fatherless boys! And so many of them wind up in prison. Boys in gangs. And the masculine women walking their pit bulls in the 90s when I came around. Such a lesbian moment for dogs. None of you had dads. You became them. Somebody had to do it.

Here's a new location. Young dog standing in a marketplace examining pair of purple shoes with turned-up toes. Shoes being extended to him. It's a gift. Dog looks out a window at a train station in Spain. The sign says Jerez. Sherry! Dog pulls at her collar which is tightening. Choked up. She doesn't know why. Barcelona. She's sitting at a lunch counter—greasy churros which she dips into her coffee. Oil dancing on the surface of her coffee in the morning light. Opens her notebook but she's got nothing to say. It's just a gleaming hole in the day. A dog can't write. No one knows she is *here*. Though silent she is quietly thrilled by her position in the world. A dog can do this. Look here. A dog has a bunk on a boat. When he closes his eyes the sea rocks and he knows he will sleep so deeply with the world swaying this way and that. There are sounds, there are tiny sounds, clunks out there, there are no sights. And there is a place for that. *For the darkness is the darkness of the dog inside the womb which is the boat.* Let me say that again: *For the darkness is the darkness of the dog inside the womb which is the boat.* Which is all the little doggies jostling into each other in the womb. No dog is born alone. A dog does not come into the room by herself. Nods. Lot of shaking going on. We love boats. The young man opens his eyes and it is Sicily rising like a cake in the air. No maybe it's Naples. The boat is landing. He better get up.

He is sitting on a boat in the harbor in Provincetown. He is drinking a cup of coffee with the crew. And those dogs wear woolen caps and have dark blue sweaters on. He would like one. A boy is drowning in Provincetown. The dog stands on the beach. He sees the boy's white hand raising above the waters and then he is gone. A girl kisses her dead mother's cheek. The coffin is shut. She will tell her puppies this same story again and again. The puppies go brrr. That's what a mother is. She tells the same story. She writes inside you. A woman is loaded on a chair into the back of a van. They could be gassing her. It's like a dog mother. For years this mother will tell the attendants all the people around her who will keep changing for years. She tells every one of them.

I want to go home,

I want to go home.

Eileen: You know I was just in Ireland and I was thinking why didn't they send her *there*. They could have just sent her back.

Rosie: I don't think they had money Eileen. May I continue.

Eileen: Sure.

A woman cries in her winged back chair and her puppy walks up and says Mommy I'm here. The woman sobs even harder. A small dog is loaded into a tiny room with other dogs who are all smashed together a big pile of them scared half to death up onto the side of the room altogether and then the gas starts pouring in. A dreaming dog cries. When you see a dog doing that paddling and the woo woo people say look *she's dreaming, she's hunting*. No she is fleeing the mass extermination of dogs. You think they don't all know it. Feel it. This happens thousands and thousands of times a day.

And the mother says there were just so many . . .

A dog runs and runs in a meadow surrounded by prancing deer bounding in and out of the woods. The dog spins around, young, not knowing which way to turn first. The strongest smell on the beach is a bell. It rings and rings. I feel it wants me to throw myself down and roll in it even though I know I can't get that rich stinky smell inside of me that way. I want it all over me. My fur is covered with mouths and noses. The smell is so cheesy and loud. It is a flag to all dogs. We love death. We love *death death death*. That's our song. It's our seasoning.

Here's a row of us with our mouths opened wide singing up along the upper left corner of the carpet. *Mille chiots*. A thousand puppies. And we sing the smell of dead birds. The smell of rats. A good dead mouth. I mean *mouse*. The pond is long. It should be . . . *here*.

Rosie makes a circle with her paw, hitting and thumping the carpet. Blue pond. No, no—*brown* pond. Brown pond. I walk around it all day. My brother and I run ahead, there's Hoover. Remember Hoover racing up and down the dunes up and down until he tore his little rear legs. He was the craziest puppy! Yet always he and I would stop and turn back to see if you were still there. Like two dog princes looking back at you and all the windows of Provincetown were pink. That's dusk. Is it sad. It's a thick stitch. Which is why we remember. Lot's wife turned into a *picture* in our heads not a pillar of salt. Sodom and Gomorrah. Pee yew. Those were happy dogs. People did just what they wanted there. It smelled very good. I know some Roman dogs too. Not the famous pair. I know Luca, you know the guy on the floor in Pompeii. He was leaping for a ball when the thing hit. He's a very good guy. Lives now in Cambridge, Mass. Professor, I think.

I'm in the barnyard now. Yeah, Pennsylvania. Baby chick in my mouth and I'm circling. I killed her accidentally. Everyone was mad. I had her in my mouth. You made me so nervous. The sky wide open. The sky is cool. The whole top of the carpet is sky. The stars are warm the closer you get but right here where you can't ever catch them they almost squeak and my paw falls into the hole of one and I'm turning around. I'm stuck but I'm turning and I'm the oldest dog up here, I am the *only* one. There's lots of holes in the tapestry. Cigarette burns. Those old kings were pigs. They would throw their old chicken bones at the tapestry. Nuts.

Here I am surfing on the wing of a plane and I have a bone in my mouth. I am total pornography. I am dog. And the stars sprout strands of wheat, weeds and flowers, the whole thing becomes day, wild tall grasses and my fur is itchy and rubbed so slightly by everything that's in the wild grass and I fall on the ground and sniff. I start to dig and I look and sniff again and I dig and now I hear someone calling. Look at this. *Look at that dog.* It's me.

Rosie's upright at a table in a nice wool suit. He's wearing a black silky tie jacket he has a striped shirt on and an untouched scone and butter sits in front of him on the table. And some glistening bacon he'd actually prefer. *Goosh.* Push the old muzzle right into the bacon and eat it all. Oh boy does he want to slobber. He sips his tea and smiles like he is sooo grateful but really he wants to howl and bark and go out into the yard and play. Wants to tear off the man clothes and bite the leg of the woman across from him smiling. I want to sniff up her skirt. I can smell her from here. That's *gooood.* She smells like the sea. I like the darkness down there. Her eyes are crazy. She has bright white hair and she is smiling and smiling because everything's hers. I know what I want. I'm a dog. Is this a dream. I'm a certain kind of husband. And there are hundreds of these men. Will we wait our whole lives to get out of this terrible joke. Life is a terrible terrible joke. Indeed. And every dog knows this. And hey-y-y-y-y. Watch the little curling vine lead right <u>there</u>. Here.

The whole ship is shaking. The panel lights flashing, numbers flipping, vanishing. My co-pilot turns and grins at me. Here we go. This is not what I imagined. Just sitting here watching it happen. I feel like a guinea pig. A pet. I have my work-suit on. A onesie with lots of pockets. I'm under this woman's sink and I think I can see where the leak is coming from. Got my paw on it. I can feel it then she stoops down next to me and asks how's it going. She's a little close. It's good I shout at the pipe. Let her think I'm crazy. It's all dark under there and the pipe is peeling. You want a beer she goes. What I yell. Not now, she says. I'm okay I yell. Do you mind if I use the toilet she asks. Uh (that's weird) go ahead. I won't look. I can hear her peeing I can even smell her pee and I can feel her smiling. She drops her hand down by my butt. Ok what's going on. She is squeezing my balls. She is so totally squeezing them. This is out of control. The spiral falls and I'm moving into the grey and green landscape with Jethro. You look depressed.

Jethro: I was.

Rosie: The beach down there is black I understand but it's also cold out. The water's cold. I don't like rain either. My nose gets cold and I wait. I rub my shoulder against your leg to tell you I'm here. My pads are chapped. Even the little sacs on the sides of my butthole are all filled from the stress. It collects. I tighten my ass in the cold. Oh yeah and I'm dead. Big deal. I rub against your familiar hand. This is beautiful. This looks so good. Iceland was a place you wanted to return. Right. This is your heart. The whole area. It's one of your dying places. All black and salty.

Is this ghostwriting.

Yeah it actually is . . . cause dog is travelling through you. I'm dead but you're *going* to be dead. The tapestry is like an advance memory. The weave knows. We feel every bump in the road, and I suppose every stitch has a smell. Otherwise *I* wouldn't know which way to go. It's a feeling thing. If a volcano's about to explode the weave expands. Something's so ready to tear it all open but it hasn't happened yet. Count to ninety it's gone.

Everything. We're very reliant on patterning. The strong dark line. The tone l-i-t-e-r-a-l-l-y holds the unicorn up. It's how she survives. Enables the *mille fleurs*. And a course *mille chiots*. The thousand puppies hold her up. And she is every gender. The famous unicorn tapestry suggests that dogs helped to kill her. A gang of skinny white dogs with hate in their eyes. It's not true. [Looks up.] We uphold her beauty. So it's an example of . . . political dishonesty. The pit bull shrugs.

In January I put my foot on the ground. I pick it right up right cause they *salt* the sidewalks in New York. In February I see you pacing . . . trying to figure out if you love enough. You don't. In March I'm wandering over mountains with goats. I'm looking at their triangle devil faces that always look like the end of the world. Know what I mean. Look at those faces. Goats are weird. I don't want that cheese.

I like the cheese.

I know. In April I'm getting shuffled from one place to the next. I'm freezing, and I don't understand where the sun is and my yard is gone. I don't know where the ocean has gone. I don't walk the beach. The rain gear's awful—doesn't fit. When I think of how unprivileged I was, how fucking poor, and now you have those two little brats. You did. That's why I don't know if Hank belongs in this book. *The little yellow dog.* Ugh. Little king. How many travelling bags does his majesty have. How much do you pay the dog-sitter. Don't you have *any friends* who like dogs. Didn't she.

Eileen: Maybe this is not the place . . .

Rosie: Oh yeah . . . very tasteful dog book. Look, we don't even know who's publishing it. I want this shit to stink of truth. I want it to *sing*. Speaking of which you know they actually made songs to go with tapestries. We should do that. I don't know. Maybe. In the songs the voices would kind of chase each other and are "accompanied by a lute played with a plectrum."

Eileen: What's a plectrum.

Rosie: I figured it was a bone.

By May everyone forgot how fast I was. I jumped up on the table and ate all the food. It was right there on plates. You were in the next room hating each other. Pit bulls are not bad. You'd do the same. Greedy pigs take everything. I'm in a box in the hold of the plane. It's freezing then it's so hot. I can't even breathe. I am dying. Let this be known. My name is Tucker, I am a Great Dane, I am six years old and I am now dead. *Thank you for this moment in eternity, Rosie.* Airlines do not like dogs. American Airlines. So sue me.

Dogs to them aren't *even* luggage. Please. Put me on a boat. Leave me home. Let me die on the street. Just never on a plane. Not me, Tucker, your big tall gorgeous baby. Dead. I wish that woman's hands were on my balls again. And I'm in a mine with a lamp on my head. That would feel great. I'm going to die. And I'm in my yard and I'm dead. And I'm watching them throw a whole lot of us, we're things now, right? . . . into the incinerator. Whose dust is whose. Cremation is a fraud and you know it. Stop that faucet from dripping. Make the snow come cause I *love* it. The wild kingdom opens in my heart in snow.

It's June. It's a waterfall. I'm on my motorcycle and I mean all summer with goggles. I wrap tape around my legs, leather tape, and I have headphones on which I know is crazy dangerous too. I'm riding up and down hills not far from the bay. I'm listening to Jeff Buckley. Hallelujah and I get pulled over. Officer I'm a dog. We're in a cartoon. There's orange dunes behind us and a smiley sun in the sky. The music is wailing. It's wiggles. You know like those rays going out. I slept with Jeff once. Well a couple of nights. Him and Rebecca. He wasn't exactly him yet

but I was Rosie. He was a kid. I don't change. I liked his smell.
Dirt under one fingernail. Jeff had a cold. I remember. I slept
with a lot of people. I lived in the era of friendship no money.
Yet I died in a state of relative wealth.

September my head's in my bowl. You think nothing ever happened to this kid. We're on the beach at Cherry Grove. Under
an umbrella. I'm little really little and a wave holds its raised
paw forever cause it's nature. Stitch o'clock. The ocean's this
blue creature growling lion it's bigger than me and I take a few
quick chubby steps back. Everyone laughs and picks me up.
I know some pictures were taken of that moment. Here they
are in my soul. Drop em in. My infinite is a permanent spot.
I rub my paw over the bumpy surface of these white clouds
of mist up there and my own wide puppy eyes one early fall
afternoon when it was still hot and circumstances and Jeanette
carried us just once to that September beach.

Pumpkins scare me. I get my kids all around me and I use the
big butcher knife and plunge it in and their little puppy eyes
are still with fear and excitement. I make a lid and I cut it out
and then I make the kids stick their paws in and pull the orange
guts out of the pumpkin. Do you want a funny pumpkin or a
sad pumpkin or a scary one. Scary they all scream. I am sitting
in school and the president is shot and we can go home early.
Get this uniform off and run naked in the yard barking and
yelling and having a ball. Do I care. I'm dirty now. Nobody
has a dad now the whole country has none but if I was there I
would have liked to seen his guts. I take a picture of that and
hold it out forever strumming and wide. Stitch some red on

his shoulder brains all polka dot and everyone returning to it again and again for years. It has to be very strong. I was in the car. Maybe I did it. What does car mean. Give me a liver chip. Give me ten. I want to fill my mouth with food. Look at me my big shark mouth full of purple food. I'm smiling. I'm history too.

I have a big thick dangling chain around my neck. With a little lock like Sid. I got used in a presidential campaign believe it or not. I'm talking to the world now. This tube puppy body, this face. And by someone so stupid when she was twelve she had a Barry Goldwater poster hanging over her Hollywood bed because it was free. Big black and orange poster. I'd like a photo of that.

I missed nothing having been free to wander through all of her eggs and cells and seeds going forwards and backwards forever. Her family of course her father back to Ireland my family any place I want to go. I'm putting pictures of him in here. And crowds of things pouring: the trellises dots and the landscapes. Guts and entrails. Finials and fruit. Futurity. We travel in dreams now. That's why I'm so relaxed.

I'm dopey cute. I look good on a button. You had that short Pekinese girlfriend she looked like a cat. She turned you on to cats. Very talented but deranged. She took the pictures and made a contact sheet of our afternoon before everything was digital. It's December. Days when I'd steal a kid's soccer ball and not give it back. What pleasure. Burst it like a grape. You bought so many. *Take your jacket off.* We're in the schoolyard on 4th St. fooling around. I was young, about a year old, and even you, Jethro, you were a lot younger. You were like forty? Look at our joy, yaps wide open laughing and gleeful—we're like World War II looking, *a sepia innocence.* Like Ewan Mac-Gregor that out-of-time joyful look. We all loved each other that day. Hard to know what's memory. The picture locks it in.

Remember Jethro and we walked to the printing shop on twenty-seventh with xeroxes of the contact sheet and circles penciled over them size of buttons and Vivien had typed slogans on them. At times it said nothing. She had an eye.

When you think of it there really could be a whole tapestry just of our presidential campaign. And because of my looks and also because of my un-conflicted attitude I had waaay more celebrity than you ever did. Ha. Pretty disgusting. Remember the guy in Washington Square Park. Hey isn't that dog running for President. And aren't *you* doing something too? That was no joke. I was on MTV. When you travelled I was home making deals in the dog run, solidifying our stance. Getting the rottweilers behind us and the labs. Jack Russells. Even those little jerks. A pit bull works. That is my thesis. And I was always a political dog.

To the Post Office

I'm on my back and you're rubbing my belly. I'm a singularity. I throw myself down on the sidewalk, start rolling, and people rub. People are not so separate. Liking is just a shape that anyone would flow around. It definitely explains popularity in art though some art some people really just love to hate.

You couldn't hate us. The smiling pictures turned up again and again. But look right here at the girl. Pure sepia. With a bow on her head. The O'Riordans—okay we're in Ireland now and the O'Riordans handed you a picture. My sister—your Aunt Helen. This tiny girl with the bow (like a little dog!) is the crux between Ireland and America. She's your father's older sister [Turn it over: *and we think she may've had an early death* . . .] now we've got every one of them sitting on the couch:

Helen

Nellie

Ellen

Eileen

Eileen Lynch says it's one name. It's all the same. Least in Irish.
Eileen's 93 years old. She's a weaver. Your great aunt Jane's girl.
Look all around *her*. Those flowers are voluminously real. *Mille
fleur*. We embroidered your own sad line right here: *I was your
unicorn but you did not protect me.* You were wounded. Okay
Ulysses. So we'll put your aunts and your sister and her wife
and your lesbian friends and your mother. Put em all right here
on the long purple dog couch. It's 2005 and the whole gang is
watching the L-word. When it was still funny. Havin' a ball.
Hooting and snacking. Women love to eat. The Irish do. In
fact they insist. A starving island has to live out. This is a very
beautiful part of the tapestry:

Helen Nellie Ellen Eileen

This is for you, Eileen but I'm thinking I'd like to stretch myself across those juicy laps least one or two. *Snort*. I'm being
obnoxious. I'm being a dog. Little hipster guy in a teeny hat.
Pal Rosie. *Doo-do-do-do-do*. I have this sexy canine swagger. I
crawl up while they're eating and watching television so they
won't even notice and maybe your Aunt Helen calls my name
(*Ro-sie!*) like I'm too big to be acting so small. *I'm a pit bull,
Sister, I'm a pup*. I'm a Staffordshire, Baby. I'm fifty, sixty pushy
pounds of doggy love. Rosie they all laugh and that fast I shoot
across three laps. I throw my paws in the air and I wriggle.
I get some food: pepperoni, cheese, mouthfuls of chips, pats
and some strokes. A pit bull is a charming homeless girl. Look
at this smile. She is <u>not</u> afflicted. She takes it close and warm.
Know, Doggies, and I'm talking to the puppies now—when
you *go* to a party just think. You're about *this* low . . .

In tall rising weeds everywhere, like a forest all the legs in the
world and especially on a big decorative rug the pup is looking
up. Looking dumb. You learn a lot about what's in the room
from this position. Mostly you're a pointer. We all have that
same cartoon job. The pup turns his head. Or maybe I just
go to bed. And everyone laughs. That's my bed right there on
the floor.

I'm off to dreamland, Kids!

*If this afternoon were forever and it's hot. And sticky and chafing
under my collar so I lift my head. I wonder if I've ruined everything by sitting next to this tree in the dark and no one can see it
or anything and it is covered soaked by rain. The whole picture's*

covered in rain. It's a wet dream. It's so long in the future already and you fall back asleep one night and inside your dream you slip off into a cave. Inside the cave is a river and a boat. You get inside the boat and you're paddling and you feel surprised to discover you're very very strong when you felt weak for so much of your life. I'm free to just love you now in here. And I will just crawl inside you. I wonder who I am you smiled. A tiny lock over a grate is baking in the sun as the east heats up and one day that lock pops open. I'm dead you realize smiling. You start rowing harder and faster than ever before. You are all the ages you've ever been. And even the earth is opening now. If there were anyone there to watch you they would see a puppy girl paddling, an old dog woman and a young female kid. Not a goat. Each of them rowing as hard as the rest. You're one person now. It's like the accordion's shut. You play that one note. One long beautiful note.

And now everything's gone—all our memories. Human history is gone. Even a tiny gravestone is covered when the monuments and boulders roof of the old medieval church and the hills and the whole world collapses widely and permanently into one crude pile. The valley is shoveling itself onto the city. There's no god, no golden foot is now making its way crunching up over the mountains of stone and the torn apart cars and bicycles and streaming water rusting them tinkling in eternity and mud splashing over the surface of an orb, O poor baby Earth, you've been alone so long. The sun comes out and then that stops. It breaks and falls like an egg. It was never light in your cave. It was always dark in there. And you never were. Something's happened. Look at the ground. It's Judgment Day. Jeesh. Look at it. And now, look—! Those ants are going to hell!

Okay you can open your eyes. The pit bull is watching the skyline. She's whispering inside my head. She's singing to me. *One tree that's all you need.* Shaped like broccoli or cauliflower some rainy day. I'm glad I woke. Maybe I'll make some coffee. She keeps whispering. *One tree.* That's all you need. Start a whole civilization that way. *One little piece grows it all.* Feel the bump. And her paw holds my fingers to the weave. I don't want to wake up. *That's it, she says.* Every part grows from every other part. *Feel it.* Every tiny leaf on the tree is singing. Can you hear it. *Yes.* Alright now.

And one day I answered the phone.

The square thing was blinking on the floor. It always was and I'd feel your feet on the stairs, the door fling open and you looked down at the thing to see what it wanted. It was a part of a phone but it felt like a bank. I was alone so much in the beginning. Once I had a whole weekend by myself and covered the apartment in poop. It looked like little piles of rope. I heard you say that when you got home. I was so scared. I heard the telephone ring. It was on the floor and I'm small, I'm wee, and I pushed the receiver off the cradle with my nose. Yes. I could not speak. Yet I was not deaf. I recognized Tom on the other side. He has a very loud voice. He knew it was me. I said err-roorahrah rah. Rah. I said erooo. I meant help me, help me. He said Rosie. I could hear him laughing. I said erroo. I'm not kidding. He didn't know what to say. You can often feel this in the human. Outside their pattern. It's all helplessness. Quiet. They don't know how to connect. They can't say errroooo. They can but they won't. But if you watch them long enough they do.

They say uh. They say mmm. They smack their tongue against the top of their mouth and hold their mouth open. They cast their eyes up. They do a deep *huh*. They shuffle the air out through their nose from the back of their throat. They take a quick breath in. They shake their head. They stomp their feet. They shake it again. They raise their eyebrows. They turn up the corner of their mouth. They suck the back of their teeth. Squeak. Like a bird sound. They sniff and then fall back in their chair. They spring forward. Nothing happens. They make these speeches all the time but they pretend it's not happening. Intuition. The silent lesson. We know what they think. They felt the pounding of feet and hoofs on the ground from great distance. Though she was born alone very often he was not. There's no way to prove the hairier ones were born in litters. In the time before ideas just drawings and sounds and she and he lived that way. She was the queen of course and he was her laborer. Her soldier and her farmer. She allowed herself to be impregnated many times. By different men. She communicated through looks what she meant and what he wanted and sometimes marks on the wall and she spoke through her eyes and the patterns of silence along the horizon. Humans were biped dogs. Are we one. I think so. In that tapestry you knew what I meant. It was the crowded room of the cave. The rain comes down and you go outside because you feel it. This is what it is to be a dog. Weather and feeling and knowing. That's why you let us remain. You love how we walk around smelling things. How we're always hungry. How we would have sex with anybody and how it's very clear who we won't have sex with. How it seems like we worship you. You love how a dog settles in and sits down. You love how a dog enters and digs. How a dog picks a place on the rug and scratches and circles around and lands and adjusts. Now I'm in the room. And now I look up. And you laugh. Why. Because of your deliberate apartness from yourself. And I always bring you back. Do you see what I mean. You wait and then you sniff.

That yellowish tree down there by the lake is waving. You think it's not communicating. Not as much as say that door down the hall. Slam. Not as much as the rooms. Go see Esther. That's what it's saying. Go see Esther. Go ahead. And you can't have the dog. You can't have Peggy. But you need to know about her. How is Peggy. How is the dog.

September 10, 2013

The dog's meat makes me sad. Why didn't I give her all the meat. All the milk—I didn't drink the milk last night when I couldn't sleep so I could have the milk now with my cereal & I don't want it. There's not enough time for anything and the sun is shining and life oh did I miss it, you, did I miss everything?

Did I miss you—oh God—

I fall into it.

I heated the lamb for the dog and I ate it. Drank the milk, scrambled the egg and ate it too. Packed the orange juice.

Good-bye and I coloured one little island out.

Tell the story of Peggy.

Okay. Peggy came to the door in the rain in September. I heard her whimpering. We will draw a small box in the bottom of the story and that area will be for Peggy's story.

I have not seen her again.

Tell the story of Peggy.

Okay. I let her in and she looked around. She was nervous. She was three colors, white black and brown. *Was she smaller than me.* She was. She was at that time but I have not seen her lately. Very large paws. Very large ears. A large wide snout of the Richard Gere variety that adds to the animal tenderness of the dark brown eyes. This brown is more of a variety of honey. She is not unlike the colours of Rosie though distributed differently. She will look well on the rug. *I agree.* Her fur was loaded with burrs and I picked each of them out. She seemed lost. She was a puppy (a large one) and it was raining out. May we have some blue rain on the tapestry. Angling down right here. Providing energy. *I agree.* Continue. I asked if she was hungry and I made her a pale yellow egg. Scrambled. She ate it nervously looking up. She liked that it was warm. More

smelly. It was not entirely clear she wanted to be inside my
small house. It isn't in New York. It was Ireland.

"Dog's Journey" is mainly written in Ireland. (dogsjourney.
com) It began in a monastery. It had a silent start. Many fine
dogs walk in Ireland. It's true. I would go to dinner and she
would wait for me outside and sometimes she was gone. I
would sit at the table and look out and several others joined
my watching and waiting and even agreed if her owner could
not be found they would "take her." This relieved me as I
was in a passage of foreign travel though I liked the dog
very much. And though she was not allowed to be at the
estate where I was staying she petitioned to enter my home
intermittently for three days and nights. I felt she was mine
especially since we slept together her with that small guilty
look on her face and ducking into the covers and suddenly
looking up as if she had somewhere else to be which for some
reason she did not return to. Each night I would go to the
dining area and it was known I was bringing food home to
her and I would feed her. I would often be given stale bread
and milk for her and it seemed strange to me that a young
dog could be expected to live on this. Does a dog love bread.
She would eat whatever I gave. And I walked around with
her and sometimes with another going to the various homes
close by where it was suspected she lived and no one claimed
her. I was beginning to take her for my own and I named her
Peggy and I put her face on social media and the decision
was applauded. But then it transpired through the kitchen,
through the women who work here: Esther and Lavinia and

Teresa who live in this town.[21] Through Esther it was discovered that a man with two sons who had recently separated from his wife had gotten Peggy for one of the boys in hopes the boy would now stay with him and I understood the ploy had not worked but his youngest son, an autistic boy it was told had claimed the dog for his own and called her Mandy. And the dog had another friend who was a lamb and the two, dog and lamb, could often be seen sitting in the middle of the street together just a dirt road not much traffic and even sitting in the field in friendship during the day while the boy was at school and the two chums kept each other company. And were referred to as the wee dog and the wee lamb. The boy at school would come home and he would be known as the wee boy and had no other name and he wanted to keep her I was told. And that would be the end except that Esther tells me that Peggy is at her door every day and she feeds the dog and at home there is no one feeding Peggy. And a man who also lives and works here (at the estate where I am staying[22]) adds delightedly that he sees the dog and the lamb sitting in the field all day as if they are happy. And the dog is small. I ask him. The dog is larger now but not so large. And through Esther I asked again if I could take Peggy home with me (to America) and the boy's older brother said no. He is my brother's dog. But he does not feed her Esther said. The older brother said that is my brother's responsibility. I

---

21. Which is Cootehill, Cavin.

22. Annaghmakerrig. The Tyrone Guthrie Center.

have told this story only to hold Peggy longer and look at her picture which is by now almost two months old.

And by the way, Peggy, I'm fairly certain, is Nellie.

Can that be true.

Yes, the dog you so badly wanted, who crawled in your bed, was in fact your paternal grandmother, Nellie O'Riordan. You needed an Irish guide. All the women in the kitchen said you should just take her because that would be the Irish way. But there's no right way or wrong way, Eileen. I've watched you spend so much time at the crossroads thinking this or that. Because of the absence of one very clear and important idea which I will now share with you: longing is not direction. It's okay to feel very sad that this dog is not in your life and you thought she would be.

To be a deep and constant well of sadness is a very real thing but it does not mean that you should go either right or left. It just means you are a well. You need to go on and especially now you need to go fast. Because you want to cover some land in the time you've got left. I need to finish this tapestry, be done with your book and resume my own travelling. Your grandmother entered into Peggy because that's what people do all the time. Become dogs. And dogs become human that way and this transmigration of souls is a very Irish thing, remarked upon persistently in literature. But it's wider than Irish or American. More ancient. And we will continue now with our weaving. Which I think you understand now is an intuition.

A dog talking inside of your head. Listen closely. And carry this message to the world. I've been other dogs. And I've been people other than your father.

I've been Mani. In fact that's why you keep getting stuck at the crossroads. Your father was stuck and so he just died, crumpled, but you, you kind of pause and scribble a bit. Or a lot. Your favorite moment in literature is when Frank O'Hara paused (did he pause) and thought *I could just make a phone call*. It was a dog thought. Robert Johnson paused. You once had a car accident listening to Robert Johnson. He is very important for you. He made a deal with the darkness at the crossroads. It is how he got so great. Like lightning hit those fingers. Give it to me he said to the devil and that's what he got. He got it by standing there in between and welcoming the darkness in. You think it's evil. It's something else. It's what's in between.

Claim it.   *Own it.*

You've heard of Manichaeism. It's the struggle between light and dark and it's very empathetic. It's very thoughtful about the pain of the light particles trapped in all things. The light just wants to get out.

I'm Mani. I painted my teachings because if you show a story it's in the day. It's not trapped in the secret place. I mean you can barely prove what I said but I had influence. In fact people generally know more about me as an anti-belief than a belief. That's okay. I take space. I take space over power any

day. My pictures had power and travelled all over the world
for about five hundred years. I was bigger after I was dead
which I think is kind of my way. And I was trapped in a cell
and I died there.

What's lost has more power than what is saved. Known to be
lost. And that tragedy fell within. And was felt within the fol-
lowers. Your mother received a letter from a woman who was
on your father's route (no. 411) in Harvard Square and after
he died she wrote your mother to say what a wonderful man
your father was. Do you remember this story?

No need to reply. I'm taking this right to the end. All of it. I'll
introduce people, I might sing a song but I'm taking it home.
I am. Here we go. You've thought about that letter so much
because your mother lost it. She never gave it a second. It was
the way she survived. She stood there wavering on a bit of scar
tissue. It was a proud stand. That was her crossroads and she
made a sound an *umph* and then she just threw it out. That
letter about him. All his letters. He's entirely gone because she
needed to keep moving or she would have spent her life at the
crossroads. And she built him up as an enormous invisible
man. A letter carrier. A monument your dad. As someone you
needed to see. You have such figures all over your family tree.
Dogs and letter carriers. Do you know why? I will tell you.
To carry the sky. Here we go. There's a particular blue, a kind
of vibrating denim that was adopted by the US postal service
in the early twentieth century and it is technically described
as "blue mixed cadet cloth." The postal uniform is one of my
favorite colours, (I Mani, I Rosie, I Terrence) being illuminated

exactly as much and precisely as little as a night sky in winter. In that struggle of night and dark this is the exact fabric that depicts a frozen moment, a snowflake moment of colour and crystallization that all dogs and precisely calibrated spiritual beings would recognize. Visually there are colors that are also tones. That's the kind of painter Mani was. He used this color sparingly. Just a woof of it. I'm not making a dog joke. *I'm making a dog joke.* It's an Iranian painter term and I was born in Persia, I spoke Syriac Aramaic but let's be Frank. I ran. I was an Iranian holy dog. My book of paintings was called the *Arzhang*. Once I was no longer seated on the holy throne in churches because I was dead the *Arzhang* would be placed there on the highest seat. It was venerated. It was open. I'm telling you this because in our time you must make a holy book. A book full of holes about time along the shapes that grace this tapestry.

Can I be Frank again. This rug.

It's a magic rug. And I am a mailman. Your father was a mailman. Your grandmother's brother Tim O'Riordan from Knocknagoun, Rylane, Cork: mailman. On the Myles side, your grandfather's younger brother came to be known as Barney from Dunmakenna, Litton, Monaghan: mailman. It is a shame, Eileen, that you are not a mailman. The dog smiles. Perhaps you are.

But the United States as we know is a very evil and accidentally spiritual country. It is a Manichean country. So accidentally pyramids speak on its money and so accidently the cadet blue of Persia a vibrating speaking color is the uniform of the common

US mailman. And your father Terrence was one. Terrence meaning tender. It's no accident. Am I still Rosie? Perhaps you should go and look out the window and see the mixed cadet blue sky. It's a magical time and a thief's time. It's little wonder that mailmen world-wide do not simply destroy the mail. In the same way that a chorus of dogs will surely defile and piss on this rug when we are done the mailman wants nothing better than to do destroy the mail. Why? All these men and woman who are carrying these bags and carriages through the streets of the world, all of them are dogs. Does this not give you a different and a better feeling about the US postal service. It was enough for you to learn that there have been mailmen going back in your family's history for as long as there was mail. As long as there was writing. The sky is full of pictures tonight. Cadet blue is made up of millions of pinpoints of light coming through from the other side. Other side of what you might ask. The holes in the tapestry and the holes in the sky are of the same ilk. It is for the purpose of reproduction. No of course there is not just one night like tonight. It has a copy. And that has a copy. It is out there somewhere. The universe is doubled.[23] I, Mani, was given prophesy by my twin. Also if you look long at the double sky, the double universe posing as one establishes a massaging effect on your optic nerve will open a sea of images which is destiny and time. It is open tonight and tonight the night after Christmas all the messages that were ever sent, will ever be sent are written in the sky. Why are the postal workers angry? It's not enough to know that they are dogs. Just last night I was told, on Christmas of all time, a sad tale. Of course

---

23. Tripled, quadrupled, foam. But we'll stick with the double.

Christmas is the saddest day of all for me because Jesus was my other. What day was Mani born? We do not know. No copy of his book the *Arzhang* exists. We hope this book will be that copy. We know that it sat on a chair and it was revered. The dogs who work for the US postal service are sending false messages and it breaks their hearts. The sad story I heard last night was that a dog (outside of the service) had been killed, had been "put down" for biting a mailman. This is a slow religious war. The dogs who have taken the bodies of mailmen either from birth or after the time of the age of 13 when a body of one with a weak nature may be intuited are the natural prey of the dogs-in-body who are loyal to *the picture* not the script. You would think then that dogs would hate writers but it is not so. Each writer is required to tell a dog's story and so dogs attach themselves to writers to spur on the ghostwriting and a writer might worry that too many dog books are being written and no one will be interested in reading hers and buying it and (obviously Mary Oliver has written a dog book) writing a dog book is hard because the writer is in servitude to the dog most clearly now.[24] The dog has been serving the writer for years, opening up her life and getting her out into the air and onto the beaches and even bringing attractive people into the unattractive life of the writer who often never goes out. And now once she/he, the writer succumbs the dog gives pictures to the writer which the writer transcribes and we are seeing it here, most particularly in the chapters x, xx, xxx, xxxx also potentially entitled transcript or Rosie at 15 now we think that

---

24. Amy Hempel has done it many times. You do it too, writer, do not be shy.

it shall be untitled and it shall be strewn[25] and that is wisdom now in particular when Eileen lays herself down horizontal like a dog so Rosie can have her say. Peggy has spoken and even the little dethroned one, Hank, he will have his say too. Perhaps on a website. Eileen has a dog soul and it is Rosie. Eileen had a dog soul and it was Taffy and Taffy died. Eileen had a dog soul and it was Walter and she gave the Walter away and let him be renamed the hideous Nike. She stood on the road like Mani and she stood too long and finally even Walter said let me go. Let's put that one right on the tapestry [paws thumping it.] Eileen, right up *here* because it was a very sad moment. You were laying on the floor by the door and you were looking in Walter's eyes and you were praying. And Walter put his paw out and he simply meant Eileen decide and you thought he meant go Eileen. You were not a free soul then, Eileen but you are free soul now and this is why you are doing this great work for us, for me, Eileen. And all dogs. I want to return to the mailman and the letter. What is a letter, Eileen. As your father is floating over the house and the child with curly hair (with an permanent, ha!) is agonizingly writing the words *I will not talk in the corridors, I will not talk in the corridors* you were beginning your weaving Eileen.

Gertrude Stein is a very great weaver. All writers who use the sonic mode in writing are returning the fruits to the cave.

We watched you smash a red clay pineapple one day in your farmhouse in Ireland, Eileen. I hoped by now you would see

---

25. Because it is liturgy.

the meaning of it. In your windswept 18th c. summer (2013) in Italy and Ireland the pineapple was following you. The pineapple is Ganesh. I, Mani, brought Ganesh into not Christianity or whatever you call the thing I was glowing in. (Jesus was one ball and I, Mani, was the other. Jesus was my brother.) The pineapple of course is a gift.

Why were you so hurriedly moving the pineapple off the windowsill one day in Ireland. Getting ready to go again I think. Once upon a time pineapples adorned your brother's bedposts. Your brother was wealthy, Eileen. It seemed that way to you as a child because he had a paper route. You do not need a man's wealth. Mani does not need Jesus Christ's fame. People say the pineapple means "WELCOME" but it also screams *riche*. Grown elsewhere; brought here by magic the pineapple is a voluminous kind of mail. It will always be delivered. The mail will find you. Whose house are you in now, Eileen. No matter. I think you linked your fate to the road in that shattered moment. You broke finally with history and its satisfied welcome. There is only comfort now in working closely with me and all the dogs tracing a path like a Johnny Appleseed of blue fruits and sonorities across the sky. But what is it about letters. For we want to tell the truth at last and not spread the same stale jokes about dogs and mailmen. You have mailmen in your family and they were dogs and all mailmen are dogs, some born and some late intuited. We call them impregnated mailmen. Letters are the cave turned inside out. Letters are the magic hidden. Am I against writing. Am I against the text. I am against the pineapple (smash. I did it.) and I am against the letter too. When they say he goes postal he is exploding

from the pressure of carrying the letter for years. Often he is a
soldier, sometimes they are women too in fact the post office is
the single greatest employer of women in the US government.
Women quickly shinny up this pole of power. The pressure of
the letter is great. The last great thing about letter writing was
cursive and it is gone. Cursive was a photograph of the nerves
of the writer. So though the load of the letter was great the
flying hand like a bird told the inside of the cave of the writer.
It is abstracted stuff. The pressure of the light particles is great
inside matter. Imagine when there are no pictures. Each letter rolls in front of a cave and shuts out the light. What else
does it do. The last great thing was the typewritten letter. The
weight of the body on the tap tap tapping machine. The choice
of paper. Often usually the hand has written the address on
the outside of the envelope. Often the body has moistened
the stamp and has stuck it on. Less involved we tear a piece
away and we stick it on now. Possibly a hair may get caught
in the pressure of that. A dirty person will leave something if
not spit. But how is the mailman against the letter itself. He
carries the world. Women too. The US post office is the most
gender-neutral division of the US government. She carries the
compacted dreams. The language implodes each time.

I have sent her thirty-six letters of my love towards the end of
a century.

My wildest love never before offered in print.

I wrote it carefully on light blue paper in India. In another
year or two in a fit of rage I sent all her letters back. And she

burned them all she said. Did she. My love and hers com-
mingled in a pile of ash in her driveway. Another time a man
took all of my young poet letters I wrote him in the 80s and
piled them in his sink and burned them. These people are sad
demons, lovers turned un-lovers. These tragedies released the
news from itself and somewhere a postal worker's burden was
lightened. The letter does not stop. You write a letter and it
goes somewhere and someone reads it and the letter goes back
and forth multitudinously. A letter will never die. It must be
burned I say to be returned to light. The post office needs to
walk in the blue uniform of time, the mixed cadet, and be seen
knowing your messages are being sent by his footsteps and by
your thought the ancient method. Dogs should wander freely
and so should the postal workers. Fed Ex is evil because it is
faster. The post office could be faster still in the Neanderthal
way of no trace. Not the toxic electronic light of the internet.
What is the internet. The observed letter. The un-private mind.
The mind will be open soon enough. The white man came in
the middle of the night and clubbed and axed the children and
the women to death. He is not worth the dogs he has working
and living with him. Each wounded space should hold a party
and it will. A letter is like a dream of a thought.

We mourn the loss of the letter but dogs mourn the loss of
the thought.

The postal uniforms could grow softer, longer and looser more
like tunics. And the post offices could each be decorated by a
tapestry such as this made by idle postal women and men no
longer on a particular route but wandering aimlessly being the

beautiful letters of our time. To be a season of postal workers
wandering in their lightweight gossamer mixed cadet blue shirts
and pants and gowns. In the winter the fine blue wool coats
reflecting the sky and when a snowflake falls on the arm of a
postal worker he will stop and smile and gesture to all around
him and they will look at what has landed on him and what is
falling in the skies because he is a dog and dogs love snow. There
is no burden anymore. Neither snow nor sleet nor rain shall be
considered anything but colors and not problems at all. What
the sky is doing that I am continuous with and look at what
has fallen on my arm. The hats of the worker will grow lush.
Wide brimmed in summer with flowers and fruits beginning to
grow off them and in winter tall feathers to communicate with
the birds flying south or staying around. Slowly the hats will
fall and drape the bodies of the postal workers and the clothes
will begin to fall away and the hair will grow wild and curly.
The women will be models for all of the other humans. Wild
strong mammalian women of the US Postal service carrying
nothing but a strong and passionate attitude and a message for
everyone which is their own bouncing back and forth among
them all for eternity or infinity or today. Time in the hands of
the postal worker will become slowly unlabeled. Fed Ex and
UPS will continue rushing around but increasingly they will
not be carrying anything except speed itself and eventually
they will begin bumping into each other and only each other
because the proper refuge will have occurred and everyone will
be beginning to live slowly in the right time with themselves.
Because there is no kingdom now and the end is only when
the road has invited us to leave. Are we ready?

The Walk

What date is it.

I don't know.

Well, guess.

August 17, 2008.

You're sure about the 2008 part.

Yes because . . .

It is. You're right.

The two kicked up dust as they walked on the path between pine trees. Occasionally the trees broke and they saw clear marsh vistas, they saw on and on to the sea. In front of them, way in front were dunes. It was hot.

I want to lie down.

That's not what you actually said.

I think they're with us.

The man was taller than the woman. He smiled at her.

Do you.

Yes, you don't feel them.

Man huffs but without ill will.

I don't know what I feel.

Well this is a séance.

That's nice. He laughs. A fire-road séance.

Do you think it's gross that I'm recording this.

You're an artist. You have to do it.

I could turn it off.

Maybe it would feel better if I turned it off.

I'm sure it's a mess.

Nothing wrong with that. People are always happy to give me their messes.

This is my mess.

He laughs. Thank you for inviting me into your mess.

I'm honored.

Really.

Seriously.

I hate these people with their actual dogs.

I hate their dogs.

Do you.

Well look at them.

Yeah those are terrible people.

People from Boston.

They look totally Boston.

How can you tell.

You can't.

I can. I mean they might be Duxbury.

Right. Duxbury. Man huffs again.

My family ruined my life going to Duxbury.

Miles Standish monument.

I don't think we ever went up.

Oh we did.

It was horrible. I think I have vertigo because of that fucking . . .

Back to the séance.

I'm doing whatever you need. I love you. I'm here because this is important to you.

She feels embarrassed. Maybe it's crazy.

Maybe it is. She likes his attitude.

What *is* his attitude.

There's Mark.

Really.

Yeah let me talk to Mark for a minute. He grins at her then goes.

She looks into the pines. She squeezes her bag. The box is there. She thinks of them joking about leaving Jimmy on the LIRR. A can of Jim. No matter how much you loved someone their ashes or just their dead body is this joke.

Ready.

Yeah what else am I going to do. She smiles at him.

Now they can see the lighthouse and the dunes. The sky is just flat blue and it's kind of buggy. Not as buggy as back there.

They reach a little bridge with running water and a tiny beach below.

Oh now I see what that's for.

Yeah I need some rocks.

The man starts picking up rocks.

Is this right.

It's a little large.

How large did she like.

She liked like this.

Unh. Okay. That's actually a hard size.

Carla invented this game.

Really.

Yeah she loved Rosie.

Until Hoover came along.

I wonder if Hoover's still around.

I don't feel it.

A whole dog generation gone.

Now why did Hoover hate Lucky.

Hoover didn't hate Lucky.

Are you kidding me.

Rosie hated Lucky because Lucky liked Hoover.

Rosie hated Hoover but Hoover was hers.

Hoover was a girl. I always forget that.

Did I say Hoover was a girl.

No but I was just thinking about it.

Yeah. I can't accept it. He was such a him.

Maybe it's the name.

No it was the attitude.

And Carla's straightness. She would have a male dog.

A really crazy barky male dog.

I loved Hoover.

Did you. I did.

Splash. Do it. It feels great.

This is her place. He gleams at her.

She throws two but it doesn't feel right. Will it feel right.

How long did you have to do this.

Until she got swimming. Until she got that light in her eyes.

It was green.

What was. The light.

It was just . . . heaven. And Carla gave it to Rosie.

She invented swimming. Splash.

She invented swimming.

Splash. In Rosie's life. This game.

Did Lucky like it here.

I guess so. I feel like I can't remember what Lucky liked.

Seriously.

Trauma.

God. That was the worst dog death of all time.

I can't even speak about it.

You wouldn't get another dog.

There's Chester.

Oh yeah. Chester.

Chester's a good boy.

Laughs. It's like sex talk.

Splash. Splash. Splash.

Is that enough.

I don't think so. I don't think she's entirely . . .

Really.

No she was difficult. I would have to go down there . . .

Let's go down.

You're right. Okay. Splash.

That was fucked.

I hope someone does this for me.

I'll do it for you.

She snorts.

Is this what you want.

Whoops. I break my skull on the rock . . . burying my dog.

Water burial.

Yeah a twofer!

Maybe it's ready.

She looks at him. Yeah I guess so. She looks at the sky which is paler.

She thinks about tonight. She clicks with her spit.

Okay baby. Rosie girl. She takes the box out of her back pack.

You got the whole thing.

Yeah I got her coffin.

Bye baby girl. The powder shifts into the green water. She dips down with her hand to move it around. It just kind of sits on a rock. That's not what she means.

C'mon swim baby.

It's just us.

She dumps more and more of the powder in the water. There aren't any clumps. Maybe this isn't even her. Bullshit.

Right? What bullshit.

No it's nice.

They stand there for a moment.

Is that all. Yeah. She tips the box and a tiny trickle falls into the water and swirls for a second and lands on a rock. She swishes it with her hand.

Bye Rosie. *And the foghorn blows.*

They look at each other and laugh.

They snort.

Our dogs.

Our dogs.

Acknowledgments

I'd like to thank the following people, places & supportive institutions: the MacDowell Colony, Kim Gordon, the Radar retreat, the Lannan Foundation, Fanny Howe, Emily DeDakis and Peter Emerson, Lewis Freedman, Leopoldine Core, Nate Lippens, Robert Marshall, UC San Diego, San Diego Women's Center, UC San Diego Rainbow graduation, Erica Kaufman, Daniel Krakauer, Glenstall Abbey, Kathleen Gaul and Ali Stewart, Michael Carroll, Virginia Center for the Arts, John Ash, Maggie Paley, Katie O'Looney, Deidre Power, Glenstal Abbey, Thurston Moore and Eva Prinz, Annamagh-kerrig (the Tyrone Guthrie Center), Paige Gratland, Anna Joy Springer, Ali Liebegott, Jennifer Firestone, the Guggenheim Foundation, Dawn Allen, Jor/dana Rosenberg, Coronado, Liz Kotz, Berkeley Eco-Poetics conference, Village Zendo, Emma Smith, Dia & the Hispanic Society, Tristan Wand, Joan Larkin, Mary McElroy and the Markeys, and Joan Riordan Scanlan, Mary Riordan Noonan, Arlene Quinlan and Eileen Lynch. Always Cathy de la Cruz, and Emma Smith, my assistant for her immense talents and huge thanks to Timothy Greenfield-Sanders and his studio for finding this image of me & Rosie and generously allowing it to be on my cover. To Emilie Stewart for her unswerving faith in this book. And finally deepest thanks to my great sweet cool & inspired editor Zachary Pace and to the most thoughtful and awake person I know, my agent PJ Mark.

Parts of this book previously appeared in the following journals and anthologies: *Fear of Language, Harvard Design Magazine, Mandorla, Aufgabe, The Empty Page/fiction inspired by Sonic Youth, Circus Book, Apology, muff magazine,* and *The New Censorship.*